国际课程数学核心词汇

唯寻国际教育 组编 ◎ 袁心莹 编著

机械工业出版社
CHINA MACHINE PRESS

本书精选国际教育数学学科的核心词汇，按照通用词汇和高频专业词汇两个部分进行讲解，涵盖 GCSE、A-Level、IB-MYP、IBDP 和 AP 等国际课程。第一部分通用词汇，涵盖近十年的考试真题中高频出现的词汇，采用字母顺序排列，单词配备词频、用法、例句、同义词和漫画等，以帮助学生熟练掌握并运用此部分词汇；第二部分高频专业词汇，是课程学习阶段的专业词汇，词汇编排与教材中的顺序保持一致，按照主题进行分类，配备 explanation、翻译、近义词、反义词、拓展词汇和图片等，帮助学生准确理解学科专业词汇，并建立用英语学习的习惯。本书采用便携开本，并配有标准英音朗读音频，愿此书能够成为学生学习数学的好帮手。

图书在版编目（CIP）数据

国际课程数学核心词汇 / 袁心莹编著 . -- 北京：机械工业出版社，2020.7（2024.10 重印）
ISBN 978-7-111-66227-3

Ⅰ . ①国… Ⅱ . ①袁… Ⅲ . ①英语—词汇—中学—教学参考资料 Ⅳ . ① G634.413

中国版本图书馆 CIP 数据核字 (2020) 第 137249 号

机械工业出版社（北京市百万庄大街 22 号 邮政编码 100037）
策划编辑：孙铁军　　　　　　　责任编辑：孙铁军
责任印制：单爱军
保定市中画美凯印刷有限公司印刷

2024 年 10 月第 1 版第 6 次印刷
105mm×175mm・7.5 印张・1 插页・322 千字
标准书号：ISBN 978-7-111-66227-3
定价：45.00 元

电话服务　　　　　　　　　　网络服务
客服电话：010-88361066　　　机　工　官　网：www.cmpbook.com
　　　　　010-88379833　　　机　工　官　博：weibo.com/cmp1952
　　　　　010-68326294　　　金　书　网：www.golden-book.com
封面无防伪标均为盗版　　机工教育服务网：www.cmpedu.com

唯寻国际教育丛书编委会

总 策 划	吴 昊　潘田翰
执行策划	蔡芷桐　李晟月
特约编辑	刘 桐　张 瑞
编　　委	芮文珍　陈 啸　袁 方
	田晓捷　袁心莹　贾茹媛
	陈博林　居佳星

推荐序
FOREWORD

2007年，我前往英国就读当地一所国际学校，开始学习A-Level课程，亲身经历了从高考体系到国际课程的转变。如果问我最大的挑战是什么，一定是使用英文来学习学术课程本身，因为不仅要适应用英文阅读、理解和回答问题，还要适应西方人不同的思维习惯和答题方式。我印象最深的就是经济这门课，每节课都有非常多的阅读，大量生词查找已经非常麻烦，定义和理论也是英文的，更别说用英文来学习英文时还会碰到意思不理解的困难了。现在回过头去翻我的经济课本还可以看到密密麻麻的批注——专业词汇量不足和词义的不理解让我在之后长达一年的学习中备受折磨。

这段学习经历也成为了我们作为国际课程亲身经历者想要制作一套专业词汇书的初衷。如果有一套书能够帮助学生按照主题和难度整理好需要的专业词汇，再辅以中英文的说明，帮助学生达到本土学生的理解水平，将大大缩短学生需要适应的时间，学生也可以更加专注在知识积累本身，而不是分心在语言理解上。

唯寻汇聚了一批最优秀的老师，他们是国际课程的亲历者，也是国内最早一批国际教育的从业者。多年来，他们积累了大量的教学经验，深谙教学知识和考试技巧。除了专业的国际课程之外，我们将陆续推出"唯寻国际教育丛书"，帮助广大的国际课程学子。这套词汇书是系列教辅书的第一套，专业词汇的部分老师们按照知识内容和出现顺序进行了编排，并遴选了核心词汇和理解有困难的词汇，再反复揣摩编排逻辑，以帮助学生更好地学习、记忆和查找。

预祝进入国际课程学习的同学们顺利迈过转轨的第一道坎，实现留学梦想！

唯寻国际教育

创始人 & 总经理

2020 年 7 月

前言
PREFACE

近年来,留学大环境利好,国内出国留学呈现低龄化的趋势,越来越多的学生选择出国读本科。国内的学生接触或进入国际初、高中课程体系后,学习资料从中文变成纯英文,这对于很多学生来说是个挑战。就数学而言,虽然需要的单词量没有别的学科多,但是只要开始学习,还是会发现一些看不懂的专有名词,别说作答,即使读懂题目也可能困难。所以,提前学习,可以让各位同学在上课以及做题的时候不再迷茫。

这就是我编写这本书的原因,让刚刚进入国际课程体系,还在过渡期的同学们可以更好地融入英文学习的环境。

为了帮助更多的同学,我们选取的词汇覆盖了从 GCSE 到 A-Level,从 IB-MYP 到 IBDP,还有 AP,所以无论你是读以上哪种课程体系,都可以使用本书来解决单词问题。

在内容的设置上,全书分为通用词汇和高频专业词汇两个部分:

第一部分通用词汇是一些比较基础的非专业词汇,选自近十年真题,我们对单词进行词频排序,从中抽选出词频高、会影响题目理解且同学不认识的单词,每个单词右边标注的数字即为词频。单词下我们提供同义词、常见用法、例句，可以强化大家记忆和理解。除此之外，在这个部分，针对一些难理解的单词我们附上了有趣的漫画，帮助同学们记忆。我们建议这部分词汇刷三遍，在单词的左侧有三个 check box，刷第一遍的时候在第一个 check box 打钩，刷第二遍时已经打钩的部分就不用再看了，以此类推。这部分看完之后，同学们不仅可以扩充词汇量，考试的时候也不用担心因为不会基础词汇而看不懂题目了。具体设置如下图：

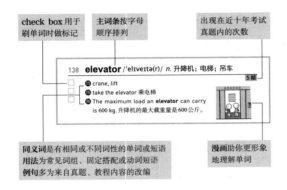

第二部分为高频专业词汇，即学科词汇，这是同学们一定要掌握的专有名词，每个单词和词组都很重要。这部分按照纯数、统计和力学分成三大模块，顺序上基本与教程内容一致，方便大家更加迅速地查找，并且更有针对性。每个单词都有中英文解释，说明其内容。其中有一些单词和词组还配有图片，方便同学们理解与记忆。另外，在选取学科词汇的时候，我们把易混淆的单词放到了一起，还为词汇配备相对应的近义词、反义词以及扩展词汇，让学生可以更加有效地记忆单词。具体设置如下图：

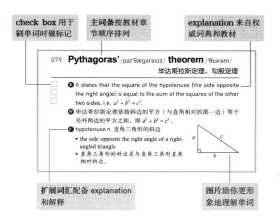

另外，全书所有单词均附有标准英音朗读音频，同学们可以扫封面或各节二维码来收听，如下图：

那么，本书怎么使用才更加高效？

通用词汇部分是每一位学生都需要掌握的词汇，在看学科词汇之前务必先把通用词汇过一遍，看是否有生词，如果有，一定消灭掉，这些是实实在在出现在真题中的词汇，同时还可以查看一下自己已有的词汇量情况。

高频专业词汇部分包括两个阶段——8~10 年级和 11~12 年级。8~10 年级的词汇是最基础的专有名词，是 GCSE 和 IB-MYP 的学生需要掌握的部分；11~12 年级的词汇则是 A-Level、IBDP 以及 AP 的学生需要掌握的部分。但如果你是体制内直接转去国际学校读 AS 或者 IBDP 的学生，那么 8~10 年级的词汇也是需要掌握的，毕竟都是学科的基础。具体说明如下：

❶ 对于 GCSE 和 IB-MYP 的学生来说，可以根据学校进度查看 8~10 年级相对应的高频专业词汇，如果程度较好，可以提前预习 11~12 年级的词汇。

❷ 对于 A-Level 的学生来说，需要先确保 8~10 年级的词汇已经掌握，再开始查看标有"仅 AP 掌握"以外的所有 11~12 年级的高频专业词汇。

❸ 对于 IBDP 的学生来说，需要掌握标有"仅 AP 掌握"以外的所有 11~12 年级的高频专业词汇。本书涵盖了 IBDP 里面前期一半左右的基本单词，后面学生熟悉了英文教学之后也就不需要单词书了。

❹ 对于 AP 的学生来说，需要掌握包括"仅 AP 掌握"的词汇在内的所有 11~12 年级的高频专业词汇，学生可以根据自己所选的科目查看并背诵单词。其中 AP Calculus 里面标有"仅 BC 掌握"是仅需要 BC

的学生掌握的单词，剩余的没有标记的是 AB 以及 BC 的学生都需要掌握的单词。

希望并相信这本诚意满满，充满硬核内容的词汇书会让同学们轻松过渡到国际课程学习！

编者

袁心莹 Wendy

2020 年 7 月

目录
CONTENTS

第一部分　通用词汇 A to Z / 1

- **A** / 2
- **B** / 11
- **C** / 14
- **D** / 25
- **E** / 30
- **F** / 35
- **G** / 38
- **H** / 40
- **I** / 42
- **J** / 48
- **K** / 49
- **L** / 50
- **M** / 51
- **N** / 55
- **O** / 56
- **P** / 59
- **Q** / 67
- **R** / 68
- **S** / 78
- **T** / 90
- **U** / 93
- **V** / 95
- **W** / 97

第二部分　高频专业词汇 / 99

第一章　8~10 年级高频专业词汇 / 100

第一节　Pure Mathematics 纯数 / 100

第一小节　Numbers 数字 / 100

第二小节　Algebra and Graph 代数和图形 / 107

第三小节　Coordinate Geometry 坐标几何 / 113
第四小节　Geometry 几何 / 117
第五小节　Measuration 测量 / 121
第六小节　Trigonometry 三角函数 / 126
第七小节　Vectors and Transformation 向量和变形 / 129

第二节　Statistics 统计 / 133

第一小节　Probability 概率 / 133
第二小节　Data Representation 数据表示法 / 136

第二章　11~12 年级高频专业词汇 / 140

第一节　Pure Mathematics 纯数 / 140

第一小节　Algebra 代数 / 140
第二小节　Functions 函数 / 142
第三小节　Trigonometry 三角函数 / 144
第四小节　Series 级数 / 147
第五小节　Differentiation and Differential Equation 微分和微分方程 / 149
第六小节　Integration 积分 / 152
第七小节　Numerical Solution and Vectors 数值解和向量 / 154
第八小节　Complex Numbers 复数 / 156
第九小节　Pre-calculus 初级微积分 ★（仅 AP 掌握）/ 159
第十小节　Calculus 微积分 ★（仅 AP 掌握）/ 161
第十一小节　Application 应用 ★（仅 AP 掌握）/ 164
第十二小节　Sequences and Series 数列和级数 ★（仅 BC 掌握）/ 166

第二节　Statistics 统计 / 169

第一小节　Representation of Data 数据表示 / 169
第二小节　Probability, Permutations and Combinations 概率、排列和组合 / 172

第三小节	Distributions 分布 / 173
第四小节	Exploring Data 探索数据 ★（仅 AP 掌握）/ 175
第五小节	Modeling Distribution of Data 数据分布建模 ★（仅 AP 掌握）/ 178
第六小节	Describing Relationship 关系描述 ★（仅 AP 掌握）/ 179
第七小节	Designing Studies 设计研究 ★（仅 AP 掌握）/ 182
第八小节	Probability and Random Variable 概率和随机变量 ★（仅 AP 掌握）/ 189
第九小节	Sampling Distribution 抽样分布 ★（仅 AP 掌握）/ 193
第十小节	Estimating with Confidence 置信估计 ★（仅 AP 掌握）/ 194
第十一小节	Testing a Claim 检验要求 ★（仅 AP 掌握）/ 196

第三节 Mechanics 力学 / 200

第一小节	Kinematics 动力学 / 200
第二小节	Force 力 / 201
第三小节	Friction and Connected Particles 摩擦和连接体 / 204
第四小节	Momentum 动量 / 206
第五小节	Work, Energy and Power 功、功率和能量 / 207

附录　高频专业词汇索引 / 210

第一部分

通用词汇 A to Z

A / 2

B / 11

C / 14

D / 25

E / 30

F / 35

G / 38

H / 40

I / 42

J / 48

K / 49

L / 50

M / 51

N / 55

O / 56

P / 59

Q / 67

R / 68

S / 78

T / 90

U / 93

V / 95

W / 97

A

扫一扫
听本节音频

001 **abroad** /əˈbrɔːd/ adv. 在国外，到海外
4频
- 用 go abroad 出国
- 例 For a holiday **abroad** you need a valid passport. 去国外度假，你需要一本有效护照。

002 **accelerate** /əkˈseləreɪt/ v. (使)加快，加速
1频
- 用 accelerate recovery 加快恢复
- 例 Exposure to the sun can **accelerate** the ageing process. 暴露在日光下会加快老化过程。

003 **acceleration** /əkˌseləˈreɪʃn/ n. 加速，加快；加速度
273频
- 用 acceleration in sth. 在某方面加速
- 例 **Acceleration** to 60 mph takes a mere 5.7 seconds. 加速到时速60英里只需5.7秒。

004 **access** /ˈækses/ n. 通道；(使用或见到的)机会，权利
vt. 存取(计算机文件)
1频
- 用 access to sth. 到某处的通道
- 例 Disabled visitors are welcome; there is good wheelchair **access** to most facilities. 欢迎残障人士参观，多数设施配有轮椅通道。

2 | 国际课程数学核心词汇

005 **accord** /əˈkɔːd/ *vt.* 给予，赠予（权力、地位、某种待遇）

1频

- 用 accord with sth. 与某事一致
- 例 These results **accord** closely with our predictions. 结果和我们的预测相当一致。

006 **account** /əˈkaʊnt/ *n.* 重要性；理由；账户

5频

- 用 take into account 考虑到
- 例 If order of choosing is not taken into **account**, the number of ways the astronauts can be chosen is 3,876. 如果不考虑选择的顺序，宇航员被选到的方法有 3,876 种。

007 **accountancy** /əˈkaʊntənsi/ *n.* 会计；会计职业

1频

- 用 accountancy firm 会计事务所
- 例 Britain is a world-class centre for the skills these new giant companies need, such as law, **accountancy** and branding. 新兴的大型公司需要诸如法律、会计和品牌创立等技术，英国在这些方面处于世界一流核心地位。

008 **accuracy** /ˈækjərəsi/ *n.* 准确（性），精确（程度）

244频

- 用 accuracy distribution 精度分配
- 例 It can be left out of the calculations without much loss of **accuracy**. 这可以被排除在计算之外，但又不会失去准确性。

009 **acknowledgement** /əkˈnɒlɪdʒmənt/ *n.* 感谢；承认

248频

- 用 in acknowledgement of 表示对……的谢意
- 例 I was sent a free copy in **acknowledgement** of my contribution. 我收到一本赠刊，表示对我投稿的谢意。

010 **actual** /ˈæktʃuəl/ *adj.* 真实的；实际的

4频

- 用 in actual fact 事实上，实际上
- 例 James looks younger than his wife but in **actual** fact he is five years older. 詹姆斯看起来比他的妻子年轻，但事实上他比妻子还要大五岁。

011 **additional** /əˈdɪʃnl/ *adj.* 额外的，外加的；附加的

359频

- 用 additional tax 附加税
- 例 The company provided **additional** £150,000 to support the project. 公司提供了额外15万英磅来支持该项目。

012 **advantage** /ədˈvɑːntɪdʒ/ *n.* 优势；有利条件（或因素）

2频

- 用 be at an advantage 处于优势
- 例 You will have an **advantage** if you have thought about the interview questions in advance. 如果你预先思考过面试问题，就会掌握优势。

013 **aeroplane** /ˈeərəpleɪn/ *n.* 飞机

8频

- 用 an aeroplane shed 飞机库
- 例 **Aeroplane** cargo faces even tighter restrictions on shape and size, not to mention the need for runways. 航空运输对货物的形状和尺寸有更加严格的限制，更不用说对跑道的依赖。

014 **aggregate** /ˈæɡrɪɡət/ *n.* 总和，总计
             adj. 总计的
            /ˈæɡrɪɡeɪt/ *vt.* 合计

4频

- 用 in (the) aggregate 总共；作为总体
- 例 Now emerging markets are in **aggregate** in surplus and the developed world is in deficit. 现在新兴市场从总体上说处于外贸盈余状态，反而发达国家处于赤字状态。

015 **aisle** /aɪl/ n. (教堂、戏院、火车等座位间的)过道，通道

3频
- 用 an aisle seat （飞机上）紧靠过道的座位
- 例 Go through every **aisle** and every corner. 穿过每条走廊，寻遍每个角落。

016 **allocate** /'æləkeɪt/ v. 拨……(给)；划……(归)；分配……(给)

4频
- 用 allocate A for B 拨 A 给 B
- 例 Each year a school **allocates** a sum of money for the library. 学校每年拨出一笔钱给图书馆。

017 **alternately** /ɔːl'tɜːnətli/ adv. 交替地；轮流地；隔一个地

3频
- 用 feel alternately hot and cold 感觉时冷时热
- 例 The ministerial conference takes place every three years in China and Africa **alternately**. 中国和非洲国家每三年轮番举办一次部长会议。

018 **alternatively** /ɔːl'tɜːnətɪvli/ adv. 要不，或者

3频
- 用 alternatively working 交替工作
- 例 **Alternatively** you could simulate the experiment on a spreadsheet. 或者，你可以在电子表格上模拟实验。

019 **altogether** /ˌɔːltə'geðə(r)/ adv. (用以强调)完全；总共；总而言之

1频
- 近 in aggregate 总计
- 用 altogether irrelevant 完全不相干
- 例 There are **altogether** 40 students in this class. 这个班总共有 40 名学生。

020 **amend** /əˈmend/ vt. 修正，修订（法律文件、声明等）

239频

- 用 amend one's ways 改过自新
- 例 In some circumstances, a party must obtain the court's permission to **amend** its complaint. 在某些情况下，当事人必须经法院许可方能修改诉讼。

021 **amount** /əˈmaʊnt/ n. 数量，数额；金额

31频

- 用 amount of sth. 某物的数量、数额
- 例 Model A assumes that the daily **amount** of growth continues to be constant at the **amount** found for the first day. 模型 A 假设每天的增长量保持在第一天的增长水平。

022 **anticlockwise** /ˌæntɪˈklɒkwaɪz/ adj. 逆时针的
adv. 逆时针地

2频

- 用 anticlockwise motion 逆时针方向运动
- 例 Turn the key **anticlockwise** / in an **anticlockwise** direction. 逆时针方向转动钥匙。

023 **apart** /əˈpɑːt/ adv. 相距；与众不同地
adj. 分离的；与众不同的

3频

- 用 apart from 除……之外尚有
- 例 Two stops on a tramline are 960 metres **apart**. 有轨电车线路的两站相距 960 米。

024 **appear** /əˈpɪə(r)/ vi. 出现；呈现

1频

- 用 appear to 出现，看来像是
- 例 The die is rolled 60 times and Janina decides that if the number 1 **appears** four times, the die must be biased. 珍妮娜断定掷 60 骰子，如果数字 1 出现 4 次，那这个骰子一定有偏差。

025 **applicant** /ˈæplɪkənt/ *n.* 申请人，候选者

3频

- 用 applicant for sth. 申请某（事）物的人
- 例 Hannah chooses 5 singers from 15 **applicants** to appear in a concert. 汉娜从十五名申请者中挑选出 5 名歌手参加音乐会。

026 **application** /ˌæplɪˈkeɪʃn/ *n.* 应用程序；应用；申请

1频

- 用 application to sb. for sth. / to do sth. 向某人申请做某事
- 例 Sandra wishes to buy some **applications** (apps) for her smartphone but she only has enough money for 5 apps in total. 桑德拉想为她的智能手机买一些应用程序，但她只有买 5 个的钱。

027 **apply** /əˈplaɪ/ *vi.* 使用；应用；申请，请求

1频

- 用 apply A to B 将 A 应用于 B
- 例 All the rules of logarithms that we have learnt so far also **apply** for natural logarithms. 到目前为止我们学过的所有对数法则也适用于自然对数。

028 **approach** /əˈprəʊtʃ/ *vi.* 接近；接洽
                                          n. 道路；手段

1频

- 同 access (*vt.* & *n.*)
- 用 approach sb. about/for sth. 为了某事（物）接触某人
- 例 Find the exact value **approached** by the mass of B as t becomes large. 求出当 t 变大时 B 的质量接近的精确值。

029 **appropriate** /əˈprəʊpriət/ *adj.* 适当的，合适的，恰当的

249频

- 用 appropriate for/to sth. 对于某物是合适的
- 例 Continuous variables, if measured accurately enough, can take any **appropriate** value. 如果连续变量测量得足够准确，则可以取任何适当的值。

030 **approximately** /əˈprɒksɪmətli/ adv. 大概，大约

4频

- 用 approximately equal 约等于，近似等于
- 例 The journey took **approximately** seven hours. 旅程大约花了7个小时。

031 **argument** /ˈɑːgjumənt/ n. 争吵，辩论；论据；论点

17频

- 用 argument for/against sth. 支持／反对某论据
- 例 After some heated **argument** a decision was finally taken. 激烈辩论后终于做出了决定。

032 **arrange** /əˈreɪndʒ/ vt. 安排；筹备；排列

4频

- 用 arrange for 为……做准备，安排，为……筹备
- 例 The party was **arranged** quickly. 聚会很快就安排好了。

033 **ascend** /əˈsend/ vi. 上升；登高

55频

- 用 in ascending order 由低到高的顺序
- 例 Obtain two results for x. One value is when the projectile is **ascending** and the other value is when it is descending. 得到 x 的两个结果，一个是抛射物上升时的值，另一个是抛射物下降时的值。

034 **assessment** /əˈsesmənt/ n. 评定，评估；看法

526频

- 用 achievement assessment 成绩评估
- 例 Objective **assessment** of the severity of the problem was difficult. 难以客观判定该问题的严重性。

035 **assume** /əˈsjuːm/ v. 假定，假设；认为

2频

- 用 assume sb. to be 假定某人是
- 例 Many of the models we have been using have **assumed** exponential growth. 我们使用的许多模型都假定了指数增长。

036 attach /əˈtætʃ/ vt. 把……固定，把……附（在……上）

98频

- 用 attach A to B 把A固定在B上
- 例 *P* is taken from the container and **attached** to one end of a light inextensible string. 从容器中取出 *P*，并将其连接到一个轻而不可伸缩绳子的一端。

037 attack /əˈtæk/ n. 进攻，攻击；袭击
v. 攻击；抨击

2频

- 用 attack on sb. 袭击某人
- 例 The patrol came under **attack** from all sides. 巡逻队受到四面八方的攻击。

038 attain /əˈteɪn/ vt. 达到；获得，得到

1频

- 用 attain to 达到，取得
- 例 The cheetah can **attain** speeds of up to 97 km/h. 猎豹的奔跑速度可达到每小时 97 公里。

039 attempt /əˈtempt/ vt. 企图；尝试
n. 企图或努力

5频

- 用 attempt to do sth. 尝试做某事
- 例 Hebe **attempts** a crossword puzzle every day. 赫柏每天都做填字游戏。

040 attraction /əˈtrækʃn/ n. 向往的地方；吸引力；有吸引力的事

1频

- 用 tourist attraction 旅游胜地
- 例 Buckingham Palace is a major tourist **attraction**. 白金汉宫是重要的旅游胜地。

041 **audience** /ˈɔːdiəns/ n. 观众，听众

5频

- 用 target audience 目标受众
- 例 The debate was televised in front of a live **audience**. 这场辩论进行了现场实况转播。

042 **avoid** /əˈvɔɪd/ vt. 避免；防止；回避

124频

- 用 avoid doing sth. 避免做某事
- 例 It is easier to show these in a separate diagram to **avoid** having to draw a three-dimensional picture. 在一个单独的图中显示这些更容易，以避免必须绘制一个三维图像。

B

043 **backpack** /ˈbækpæk/ *n.* 双肩背包，背包

3频

- 用 **backpack** camera 背包式电视摄像机
- 例 Find the probability that, in a full minibus travelling to London, between 8 passengers and 10 passengers inclusive carry a **backpack**. 求一辆满载乘客前往伦敦的小型巴士上，有 8 至 10 名乘客携带背包的概率。

044 **barrier** /ˈbæriə(r)/ *n.* 屏障；分界线；隔阂

1频

- 用 **barrier** between A and B A 与 B 之间的分界线
- 例 The Yangtze River is a natural **barrier** to the north-east. 长江是东北方向的一道天然屏障。

045 **batch** /bætʃ/ *n.* 一批；一批的生产量

1频

- 用 in **batches** 分批
- 例 In a **batch** of 300 denim jeans produced by a new employee, five are found to have faults. 在新员工加工的一批 300 条牛仔裤中，5 条被发现有瑕疵。

046 **bead** /biːd/ *n.* （液体的）小滴；（有孔的）珠子

6频

- 用 a **beaded** handbag 饰有小珠的手提包
- 例 There were **beads** of sweat on his forehead. 他的脑门上都是汗珠。

047 **biologist** /baɪˈɒlədʒɪst/ n. 生物学家

2频

- 用 marine biologist 海洋生物学家
- 例 Every time a **biologist** discovers a new species, there is the opportunity to honour someone or something. 每次生物学家发现一个新物种，就又有了一个纪念人或事的机会。

048 **block** /blɒk/ n.（方形平面）大块；立方体；街区

161频

- 用 a set of blocks 一组积木
- 例 We can see that two **blocks** represent one athlete in the histogram. 我们可以看到在直方图中两个方块代表一个运动员。

049 **boil** /bɔɪl/ v. 煮沸；（使）沸腾，达到沸点
n. 沸点

2频

- 用 boil over 沸溢；发怒
- 例 **Boil** plenty of salted water, then add the spaghetti. 把足量的盐水烧开，再放入意大利面。

050 **bounce** /baʊns/ vi.（使）弹起，弹跳；反射

2频

- 用 bounce back 恢复健康（或信心等）；重整旗鼓
- 例 The particle comes to instantaneous rest t seconds after it **bounces** on the bottom of the tank. 质点反弹到容器底部后的瞬间静止时间为 t 秒。

051 **bracket** /ˈbrækɪt/ n. 托架；支架；括号

244频

- 用 bracket sth. with sth. 把……和……归在一起
- 例 A scaffold pole of length 5 m has **brackets** bolted to it. 一个长度为 5 米的脚手架上固定了托架。

052 **brand** /brænd/ *n.* 品牌；类型

241 频

[用] brand loyalty 品牌忠诚度

[例] A **brand** of laptop battery has a lifetime of 10 years. 一个品牌的笔记本电脑电池的寿命是 10 年。

053 **briefly** /'briːfli/ *adv.* 简略地；短暂地；暂时地

2 频

[同] momently, tentatively

[用] briefly explain 简要说明

[例] We will **briefly** mention a couple of complex methods, but then go into details about the simplest method. 我们将简单提到几个复杂的方法，然后会详细介绍一个最简单的方法。

054 **bulb** /bʌlb/ *n.* 电灯泡；(植物)鳞茎

3 频

[用] bulb of the eye 眼球

[例] The **bulb** will go on sale this year. 这款灯泡将在今年上市销售。

055 **bunch** /bʌntʃ/ *n.* 束，串；大量

2 频

[用] a whole bunch of 一大堆

[例] A **bunch** of flowers consists of a mixture of roses, tulips and daffodils. 一束花由玫瑰、郁金香和水仙组成。

C

扫一扫
听本节音频

056 **cable** /ˈkeɪbl/ *n.* 电缆；(系船用的)缆绳；(支撑桥梁等用的)钢索

8频
- 用 overhead/underground cables 高架／地下电缆
- 例 The **cable** is horizontal, and the other end is attached to a 20-tonne truck. 电缆是水平的，另一端连接在 20 吨的卡车上。

057 **calculator** /ˈkælkjuleɪtə(r)/ *n.* 计算器

283频
- 用 a pocket calculator 袖珍计算器
- 例 You can use a **calculator** to add and subtract matrices of the same order and to multiply a matrix by a number. 你可以用计算器来计算同阶矩阵的加减法以及将一个矩阵乘以一个数字。

058 **candidate** /ˈkændɪdət, ˈkændɪdeɪt/ *n.* 应试者；候选人；申请人

363频
- 同 applicant
- 用 candidate for 申请人，候选人；被认定合适者
- 例 A **candidate** is chosen at random. 应试者是随机挑选的。

059 **capacity** /kəˈpæsəti/ *n.* 容量，容积；领悟(或理解、办事)能力

4频
- 用 capacity for doing sth. 办事能力
- 例 The number of people a football stadium can hold is called the '**capacity**'. 一个足球场能容纳多少人被称为"容量"。

060 **capital** /ˈkæpɪtl/ *adj.* 大写的
n. 首都；资本；财产

2频

- 用 social capital 社会资本
- 例 The password must include at least one **capital** letter, at least one digit and at least one symbol. 密码必须包含至少一个大写字母、一个数字和一个符号。

061 **category** /ˈkætəgəri/ *n.* （人或事物的）类别，种类

4频

- 近 variety, classification, kind
- 用 product category 产品类别
- 例 The results can be divided into three main **categories**. 结果可分为三大类。

062 **ceiling** /ˈsiːlɪŋ/ *n.* 天花板

1频

- 用 glass ceiling 玻璃天花板（女性或少数弱势群体在职场中难以获得晋升的一种无形的阻碍）
- 例 The other end of the string is attached to a fixed point on the **ceiling**. 绳子的另一端固定在天花板的一个固定点上。

063 **cell** /sel/ *n.* 手机；细胞；蜂房的巢室

7频

- 用 cell phone 手机
- 例 It was found that 68% of the passengers on a train used a **cell** phone during their train journey. 调查发现，火车上有 68% 的乘客在旅途中使用手机。

064 **certificate** /səˈtɪfɪkət/ *n.* 文凭，结业证书；证书

98频

- 用 a birth certificate 出生证明
- 例 He was afforded a **certificate** upon completion of his course of study. 完成课程学习后，他被授予了结业证书。

065　champion /'tʃæmpiən/ n. 冠军，优胜者
　　　　　　　　　　　　　　 vt. 捍卫，声援

4频

- 用 defending champion 卫冕冠军
- 例 He succeeded in his efforts to get the **champion**. 他经过努力，终于成功夺得了冠军。

066　chess /tʃes/ n. 国际象棋

2频

- 用 play chess 下棋
- 例 A **chess** team of 2 girls and 2 boys is to be chosen from the 7 girls and 6 boys in the chess club. 国际象棋队将从国际象棋俱乐部的7名女生和6名男生里选出两名女生和两名男生。

067　circle /'sɜːkl/ n. 圆形
　　　　　　　　　　 v. 盘旋；圈出

96频

- 用 vicious circle 恶性循环；（逻辑学）循环论证法
- 例 **Circles** are one of a collection of mathematical shapes called conics or conic sections. 圆是一组被称为圆锥或圆锥截面的数学形状的集合。

068　circular /'sɜːkjələ(r)/ adj. 圆形的，环形的

18频

- 用 circular arc 圆弧
- 例 The diagram shows a solid cylinder standing on a horizontal **circular** base with centre O and radius 4 units. 该图展示了一个实心圆柱，它位于一个水平的圆形底座上，底座圆心为O，半径为4。

069　circumference /sə'kʌmfərəns/ n. 圆周；圆周长

16频

- 用 waist circumference 腰围
- 例 The earth is almost 25,000 miles in **circumference**. 地球的周长大约为25,000英里。

070 **claim** /kleɪm/ v. 宣称 vt. 索取；认领
n. 宣称

2频

- 用 lay claim to sth. 声称对某物有所有权
- 例 Scientists are **claiming** a major breakthrough in the fight against cancer. 科学家们宣称攻克癌症已有重大的突破。

071 **client** /ˈklaɪənt/ n. 当事人；委托人；客户

11频

- 同 buyer, customer, patron, purchaser
- 用 client agreement 客户协议
- 例 Social workers must always consider the best interests of their **clients**. 社会工作者必须时刻考虑其当事人的最佳利益。

072 **cliff** /klɪf/ n. 悬崖，峭壁

5频

- 同 glacial cliff 冰崖
- 例 The top of a **cliff** is 40 metres above the level of the sea. 悬崖的顶端高出海平面 40 米。

073 **coaster** /ˈkəʊstə(r)/ n. 航行于沿海港口间的轮船；沿海航行者；过山车

7频

- 用 a roller coaster 过山车
- 例 Each British **coaster** has a salt-caked smokestack. 每艘英国沿海轮船都有一个盐饼状的大烟囱。

074 **collide** /kəˈlaɪd/ v. 碰撞；冲突；抵触

5频

- 用 collide with sb. over sth. 与某人在某事上发生冲突
- 例 The car **collided** head-on with the van. 那辆小轿车与货车迎面相撞。

075 **collision** /kəˈlɪʒn/ n. 碰撞；(意见或看法)冲突

1频

- 用 in collision 相撞；在冲突中
- 例 Stewart was injured in a **collision** with another player. 斯图尔特在与另一选手的相撞中受了伤。

076 **column** /ˈkɒləm/ *n.* 圆柱状物，柱形物；(报刊的)专栏

1频

- 用 column vector 列向量
- 例 Calculate the frequencies represented by each of the four histogram **columns**. 计算四列柱状图中每一列所代表的频率。

077 **committee** /kəˈmɪti/ *n.* 委员会

17频

- 用 Standing Committee 常委会
- 例 A **committee** of 6 people is to be chosen at random from 7 men and 9 women. 委员会中的6名成员是从7名男士和9名女士中随机挑选出来的。

078 **comparison** /kəmˈpærɪsn/ *n.* 比较，对比

1频

- 用 by comparison 相比之下
- 例 It is difficult to make a **comparison** with her previous book—they are completely different. 这很难与她以前的书相比——两者是截然不同的。

079 **compete** /kəmˈpiːt/ *vi.* 参加比赛(或竞赛)；竞争，对抗

1频

- 用 compete with/against sb. for sth. 与某人就某事展开竞争
- 例 Two heavyweight boxers decide that they would be more successful if they **competed** in a lightweight class. 两位重量级拳击手认为，如果他们参加的是轻量级别的比赛，他们会更加成功。

080 **competition** /ˌkɒmpəˈtɪʃn/ *n.* 比赛，竞赛；竞争

1频

- 同 in competition with sth. 和……竞争；与……角逐
- 例 University students from all around the country brought their android friends to participate in the **competition**. 来自全国各地的大学生们带着他们的机器人参加本次比赛。

081 **complete** /kəmˈpliːt/ *vt.* 完成；填写（表格）
adj. 彻底的，全部的

1频
- 同 accomplish, achieve, carry out
- 用 a complete change 彻底的变化
- 例 A cyclist **completes** a long-distance charity event across Africa. 一名自行车手完成了穿越非洲的长途慈善活动。

082 **component** /kəmˈpəʊnənt/ *n.* 组件；组成部分；成分

13频
- 用 component diagram 组件图
- 例 If you know the directions in which these **components** act, it is easy to construct the force diagram in reverse. 如果你知道这些组件作用的方向，则很容易反向构造出受力分析图。

083 **conditional** /kənˈdɪʃənl/ *adj.* 附带条件的，假定的；依……而定

1频
- 用 conditional probability 条件概率
- 例 Payment is **conditional** upon delivery of the goods. 货到付款。

084 **cone** /kəʊn/ *n.*（实心或空心的）圆锥体

2频
- 用 cone angle 锥角
- 例 A conic section is a curve obtained from the intersection of a plane with a **cone**. 圆锥曲线是由平面与圆锥相交而得到的曲线。

085 **consecutive** /kənˈsekjətɪv/ *adj.* 连续的

4频
- 用 consecutive reaction 连锁反应
- 例 Find by calculation the pair of **consecutive** integers between which a lies. 通过计算求 a 所在的连续整数对。

086 consist /kənˈsɪst/ vi. 由……组成（或构成）；存在于，在于

2频

- 搭 consist of 组成
- 例 This **consists** of category names and the observed frequencies. 这包含类别名称和观察次数。

087 construct /kənˈstrʌkt/ vt. （按照数学规则）绘制；建造；组成

3频

- 搭 construct A from B 用 B 建造 A
- 例 It is possible to **construct** one-sided or two-sided confidence intervals. 可以绘制出单边或双边的置信区间。

088 consumption /kənˈsʌmpʃn/ n. 消耗，消耗量；消费

2频

- 搭 energy consumption 能量损耗
- 例 Gas and oil **consumption** always increases in cold weather. 燃气和燃油的消耗量总会在天冷时增加。

089 content /ˈkɒntent/ n. 含量，容量；内容
/kənˈtent/ adj. 满意

3频

- 同 capacity (n.)
- 搭 be content with sth. 对某事（物）满意
- 例 Seventy samples of fertiliser were collected and the nitrogen **content** was measured for each sample. 收集 70 份肥料样本，并测量了每个样品的氮含量。

090 continuation /kənˌtɪnjuˈeɪʃn/ n. 附加物；连续，持续

25频

- 同 additional (adj.)
- 搭 continuation column 连续列
- 例 If you need additional answer paper or graph paper, ask the invigilator for a **continuation** booklet or graph paper booklet. 如果你需要额外的答题纸或坐标纸，可以向监考人员要附加的手册或坐标纸手册。

091 **continue** /kən'tɪnjuː/ v. 继续；持续存在；继续坚持

1频

- 用 continue the investigation 继续调查
- 例 The resistance to motion of RN **continues** to act. RN 的运动阻力继续发挥作用。

092 **continuous** /kən'tɪnjuəs/ adj. 连续的，不断的，持续的

8频

- 同 consecutive
- 用 a continuous line of traffic 络绎不绝的车辆
- 例 The **continuous** random variable X represents the error in millimetres of the actual length of a plank coming off the machine. 连续随机变量 X 表示从机器上下来的木板的实际长度的误差，单位是毫米。

093 **continuously** /kən'tɪnjuəsli/ adv. 连续不断地

1频

- 同 consecutive (adj.)
- 用 fire continuously 不断射击
- 例 Processes need to be tailored not only for each project, but also **continuously** throughout the project lifecycle. 过程不仅需要适应每个项目的不同需求，还应在项目生命周期中不断地调整。

094 **conventional** /kən'venʃnl/ adj. 常规的，依照惯例的；传统的

3频

- 同 traditional
- 用 conventional art 传统艺术
- 例 It is **conventional**, and useful, to add the row and column totals in a contingency table; these are called the marginal totals of the table. 在列表中添加行和列的总量是常规惯例，也是有用的；这些被称为表格的边际总数。

095 **converge** /kən'vɜːdʒ/ vi. 收敛，集中，汇集

2频

- 用 converge with social media 与社交媒体融合
- 例 This geometric progression **converges** to 2. 这个等比数列是趋近于 2 的。

096 **convergent** /kən'vɜːdʒnt/ adj. 收敛的；趋同的，求同的

3频
- 用 convergent evolution 趋同进化
- 例 Two **convergent** geometric progressions, P and Q, have the same sum to infinity. 两个收敛的几何级数，P 和 Q，有相同的无限项之和。

097 **coordinate** /kəʊ'ɔːdɪnət/ n. 坐标
/kəʊ'ɔːdɪneɪt/ vt. 使协调，使相配合

197频
- 用 coordinate axis 坐标轴
- 例 Write down the **coordinates** of the position of the projectile after time t. 写下时间 t 后抛射物所在的位置坐标。

098 **corner** /'kɔːnə(r)/ n. 角；角落
vt. 逼入角落

1频
- 用 around the corner 在拐角处；即将来临
- 例 In this example, you will learn how to add content, such as an image URL for your company's logo, to the right **corner** of every page. 在本例中，您将学到如何添加内容，例如，在每个页面的右下角，为您公司的图标添加一个图片地址。

099 **correction** /kə'rekʃn/ n. 修正，纠正，校正

227频
- 用 continuity correction 连续校正
- 例 Do not use staples, paper clips, glue or **correction** fluid. 不要使用订书钉、回形针、胶水或者涂改液。

100 **corresponding** /ˌkɒrə'spɒndɪŋ/ adj. 相应的，对应的；负责通讯的

6频
- 用 a corresponding secretary 负责通信的秘书
- 例 State the **corresponding** result obtained by equating the imaginary parts. 用虚数部分相等的方法得出相应的结果。

101 **count** /kaʊnt/ v. 数数；计算
n. 计算；总数

1频
- 同 aggregate (v. & n.)
- 用 count from A to B 从 A 数到 B
- 例 We can collect data by gathering and **counting**, taking surveys, giving out questionnaires or by taking measurements. 我们可以通过采集、计数、调查、发放问卷或测量的方式来收集数据。

102 **couple** /ˈkʌpl/ n. 夫妻；两人，两件事物

1频
- 用 a couple of days 一两天
- 例 These 12 passengers consist of 2 married **couples** (Mr. and Mrs. Lin and Mr. and Mrs. Brown), 5 students and 3 business people. 12 名乘客当中有两对夫妻（林先生和林太太，布朗先生和布朗太太），5 名学生和 3 名商务人士。

103 **crane** /kreɪn/ n. 起重机

6频
- 用 boom crane 吊杆起重机
- 例 A **crane** is used to raise a block of mass 50 kg vertically upwards at constant speed through a height of 3.5 m. 起重机通常可以匀速垂直地将 50 千克的重物吊到 3.5 米的高度。

104 **cumulative** /ˈkjuːmjələtɪv/ adj. 累积的

38频
- 用 cumulative effect 日积月累的影响
- 例 The **cumulative** frequency table shows the number of pupils in a school and the corresponding number of schools. 累积频率表显示出了一所学校的学生人数和相应的学校数量。

105 **customer** /ˈkʌstəmə(r)/ n. 顾客，客户

8频
- 同 client
- 用 customer value 客户价值
- 例 The firm has an excellent **customer** service department. 这家公司有非常出色的客户服务部。

106 **cycle** /ˈsaɪkl/ *n.* 循环，周期；自行车

8 频

- ⊕ life cycle 寿命周期，生存期
- ⑩ One of these branches leads to another iteration of the **cycle**. 其中一个分支引发了另一次循环的迭代。

107 **cyclist** /ˈsaɪklɪst/ *n.* 骑自行车的人

66 频

- ⊕ trick cyclist 特技自行车手
- ⑩ One of them called the policeman, one dialed 120. And the others were taking care of the **cyclist**. 他们其中一人拨打电话报警，另外一人拨打了120，其余的人在照顾受伤的骑行者。

D

108 **decelerate** /ˌdiːˈseləreɪt/ v. 减速

1 频

- 反 accelerate v. 加速
- 用 decelerate the speed 减速
- 例 Economic growth **decelerated** sharply in June. 六月份经济增长大幅减缓。

109 **deceleration** /ˌdiːseləˈreɪʃn/ n. 减速

22 频

- 反 acceleration n. 加速
- 用 deceleration force 减速力
- 例 The lift then travels for 6 s at constant speed and finally slows down, with a constant **deceleration**, stopping in a further 4 s. 然后电梯以匀速运行 6 秒,最后匀速减速,4 秒之后停止。

110 **decrease** /dɪˈkriːs/ v. 减少,降低
n. 减少量,减少

1 频

- 同 diminish (v.), lessen (v.), reduce (v.)
- 用 on the decrease 正在减少
- 例 The speed of the car increases to a maximum, then **decreases** until the car is at rest at B. 汽车的速度增加到最大值,然后减速,直到汽车在 B 处停下。

111 **degree** /dɪˈɡriː/ n. 学位;度数;程度

247 频

- 用 to a degree 在某种程度上
- 例 At company V, 12.5% of the employees have a university **degree**. 在 V 公司, 12.5% 的员工拥有大学学位。

112 deliver /dɪˈlɪvə(r)/ vt. 传送，递送，交付

1频

- 用 deliver sth. to sb. 把某物交托给某人
- 例 A free newspaper is **delivered** on Monday to 3 different houses chosen at random from these 12. 周一有一份免费的报纸会被送往 3 个不同的家庭，这 3 个家庭是从 12 个家庭中随机挑选的。

113 density /ˈdensəti/ n. 密度

5频

- 用 density function 密度函数
- 例 A histogram is drawn with a scale of 1 cm to 1 unit on the vertical axis, which represents frequency **density**. 在纵坐标上以 1 厘米为单位绘制直方图，表示频率密度。

114 department /dɪˈpɑːtmənt/ n. 部，系；(医院的)科

239频

- 同 ministry, division
- 用 marketing department 市场部
- 例 A university librarian selects a random sample of seven students from the physics **department** and records the number of books each student borrows in a particular month. 一位大学图书管理员从物理系随机挑选了 7 名学生，并记录每个学生在一个月里借阅了多少本书。

115 depend /dɪˈpend/ vi. 依赖，依靠；取决于

1频

- 用 depend on 取决于
- 例 These gem stones are sorted into three categories for sale **depending** on their weights. 这些宝石依据不同的重量被分为三类出售。

116 depth /depθ/ n. 深度，纵深

13频

- 用 in the depth of winter/despair 隆冬时节 / 处于绝望的深渊
- 例 The **depth** of the liquid in the container is 3.6 m. 容器内液体的深度为 3.6 米。

117 **derive** /dɪˈraɪv/ vi. 起源

2频

- 用 derive from 源自于
- 例 Two iterative formulae, A and B, are **derived** from this equation. 由该方程导出两个迭代公式 A 和 B。

118 **descend** /dɪˈsend/ vi. 下降，下去

2频

- 反 ascend vi. 上升，登高
- 用 descend on sth. 突然涌入；突然蜂拥而至
- 例 Find the horizontal distance from O when the particle is 2 m above the ground and **descending**. 当质点距地面 2 米并下降时，求出从 O 开始的水平距离。

119 **deviate** /ˈdiːvieɪt/ vi. 偏离；背离；违背

1频

- 用 deviate from sth. 偏离某物
- 例 He never **deviated** from his original plan. 他从未偏离最初的计划。

120 **deviation** /ˌdiːviˈeɪʃn/ n. 偏差，偏离

136频

- 用 standard deviation 标准偏差
- 例 Find the standard **deviation** of the times spent by people visiting this dentist. 计算出看此牙医的人花费时间的标准偏差。

121 **diagonal** /daɪˈæɡənl/ n. 对角线，斜线

2频

- 用 diagonal stay 斜撑杆
- 例 The **diagonals** AC and BD intersect at M. 对角线 AC 和 BD 相交于 M 点。

122 **dice** /daɪs/ n. 骰子

27频

- 用 roll/throw/shake the dice 掷/投/摇骰子
- 例 Suppose you have a set of **dice** numbered 1 to 6. 假设你有一组骰子，编号从 1 到 6。

123 **difficulty** /ˈdɪfɪkəlti/ *n.* 困难，难题

- 用 in difficulty 处境困难
- 例 A man in a boat, close to the bottom of the cliff, is in **difficulty** and fires a distress signal vertically upwards from sea level. 一名男子在靠近悬崖底部的船上遇到了困难，他从海平面垂直向上发射了遇险信号。

124 **disclosure** /dɪsˈkləʊʒə(r)/ *n.* 揭露，透露，公开

- 同 revelation
- 用 financial disclosure 财务公开
- 例 The first step for any regulator of the industry should be to demand more **disclosure**. 对于行业的任何监管机构来说，第一步都要求披露更多信息。

125 **discrete** /dɪˈskriːt/ *adj.* 离散的，不连续的

- 同 separate
- 用 discrete events 不相关的事件
- 例 In *Probability and Statistics 1*, you learnt about **discrete** probability distributions. 在《概率与统计1》中，你们学习了离散概率分布。

126 **disease** /dɪˈziːz/ *n.* 病，疾病

- 同 illness
- 用 respiratory disease 呼吸疾病
- 例 The **disease** is quickly spreading in the world. 这种疾病正迅速地向世界各地蔓延。

127 **displacement** /dɪsˈpleɪsmənt/ *n.* 位移，取代

- 用 angular displacement 角位移，角移
- 例 The **displacement** of Q from O is 400 m when $t = 10$. 当 $t = 10$ 时，从 O 到 Q 的位移为 400 米。

128 **display** /dɪˈspleɪ/ *vt.* 显示，陈列，展出

3频

- 回 exhibit
- 用 display sth. to sb. 向某人展示某物
- 例 In Chapter 1 of *Probability and Statistics 1*, the histogram was introduced as an appropriate way to **display** continuous data. 在《概率与统计1》的第一章中，介绍了图这种展示连续数据的恰当方法。

129 **distribution** /ˌdɪstrɪˈbjuːʃn/ *n.* 分布，分配

131频

- 回 allocation, assignment
- 用 distribution center 物流中心
- 例 The lengths of body feathers of a particular species of bird are modelled by a normal **distribution**. 通过正态分布对一特定鸟类的体羽长度进行建模。

130 **document** /ˈdɒkjumənt/ *n.* 文件，公文

244频

- 回 file, paper
- 用 public document 公文
- 例 This **document** consists of 3 printed pages and 1 blank page. 本文件由3页打印纸和1页空白页组成。

131 **domain** /dəˈmeɪn/ *n.* 定义域，区域；范畴

28频

- 用 domain of quantification 量化域
- 例 Find an expression for $f(x)$ and state the **domain** of f. 求出 $f(x)$ 的表达式，并给出 f 的定义域。

132 **downward** /ˈdaʊnwəd/ *adv.* 向下
                                           adj. 向下的，下降的

2频

- 回 descend (*v.*)
- 反 upward *adv.* 向上
- 用 a downward trend 下降趋势；衰退趋势
- 例 Since the force of gravity acts **downward** on the particle, its equilibrium position will be below the mid-point of *AB*. 由于重力向下作用于质点上，所以它的平衡位置在 *AB* 的中点下面。

E

133 **economy** /ɪˈkɒnəmi/ *n.* 经济，节约

3频

- 回 saving
- 用 economy with words 惜字如金
- 例 Over a period of time Julian finds that on long-distance flights he flies **economy** class on 82% of flights. 经过一段时间，朱利安发现，在他乘坐的长途航班中，有82%乘坐的是经济舱。

134 **edge** /edʒ/ *n.* 边缘，边线

22频

- 用 on the edge of sth. 在某物的边缘；濒临
- 例 Particle A is held at rest on a rough horizontal table with the string passing over a smooth pulley fixed at the **edge** of the table. 质点 A 静止在水平粗糙的桌面上，它与一根穿过桌边滑轮的细绳相连。

135 **effect** /ɪˈfekt/ *n.* 结果；影响；效应

1频

- 用 have a bad effect on sb./sth. 对某人或某物有负面影响
- 例 The **effect** is that the resultant force is unchanged in magnitude but reversed in direction. 结果是合力的大小不变，但方向相反。

136 **elapse** /ɪˈlæps/ *vi.* (时间)消逝，流逝

3频

- 回 go by
- 用 elapsed time 经过的时间
- 例 Some adults and some children each tried to estimate, without using a watch, the number of seconds that had **elapsed** in a fixed time-interval. 一些成年人和儿童都试图在不使用手表的情况下估算在固定时间间隔内的秒数。

137 **electronic** /ɪˌlek'trɒnɪk/ *adj.* 电子的，电子设备的

244 频

- 用 **electronic** commerce 电子商务
- 例 A factory makes **electronic** circuit boards and, on average, 0.3% of them have a minor fault. 一家制造电子电路板的工厂里，通常 0.3% 的电路板有小故障。

138 **elevator** /'elɪveɪtə(r)/ *n.* 升降机；电梯；吊车

5 频

- 同 crane, lift
- 用 take the elevator 乘电梯
- 例 The maximum load an **elevator** can carry is 600 kg. 升降机的最大载重量是 600 公斤。

139 **engine** /'endʒɪn/ *n.* 发动机，引擎

85 频

- 用 search **engine** 搜索引擎
- 例 On this section of the road the power of the lorry's **engine** is constant and equal to 144 kW. 在这段路上，卡车引擎的功率是恒定的，等于 144 千瓦。

140 **equidistant** /ˌiːkwɪ'dɪstənt/ *adj.* 等距的，等距

1 频

- 同 isometric
- 用 be **equidistant** from A. and B. 从 A 地到 B 地距离相等
- 例 My house is **equidistant** from the pub and the hotel. 我家离酒吧和酒店的距离相等。

141 **equilateral** /ˌiːkwɪ'lætərəl/ *adj.* 等边的 *n.* 等边形

4 频

- 用 an **equilateral** triangle 等边三角形
- 例 It is an **equilateral** triangle of side 4 cm. 这是一个边长为 4 厘米的等边三角形。

142 **equilibrium** /ˌiːkwɪ'lɪbriəm/ *n.* 平衡，均衡

86 频

- 用 dynamic **equilibrium** 动态平衡
- 例 The ring is in limiting **equilibrium**. 这个环处于极限平衡状态下。

143 equipment /ɪˈkwɪpmənt/ n. 器材，设备

- 同 facility
- 用 skiing equipment 滑雪装备
- 例 The numbers of pieces of **equipment** in each of 3 playgrounds are as follows. 3 个操场的器材件数如下。

6 频

144 estimate /ˈestɪmət/ n.（对数量，成本的）估计
/ˈestɪmeɪt/ vt. 估价，估算

- 用 cost estimate 成本估算
- 例 Their **estimates** are shown below. 他们的估数如下。

48 频

145 evaluate /ɪˈvæljueɪt/ vt. 评估，估价，估计

- 同 assessment (n.), estimate, assess
- 用 evaluate sb. on sth. 根据某事评价某人
- 例 Our research attempts to **evaluate** the effectiveness of the different drugs. 我们的研究试图评估不同药物的疗效。

7 频

146 exactly /ɪɡˈzæktli/ adv. 恰好地，精确地，准确地

- 同 accuracy (n.), precisely
- 用 exactly divisible 整除
- 例 Each of these 160 students is studying **exactly** one of these subjects. 这 160 名学生中的每一位都只学一门课程。

63 频

147 exceed /ɪkˈsiːd/ vt. 超过（数量）

- 用 exceed in... 在某方面超过
- 例 This model predicts that R cannot **exceed** a certain amount. 这个模型预测 R 不能超过一定的量。

1 频

148 exchange /ɪksˈtʃeɪndʒ/ vt. 交换，交流

- 用 exchange sth. with sb. 与某人交换某物
- 例 The forces of magnitudes 4 N and 16 N **exchange** their directions and the forces of magnitudes 8 N and 12 N also **exchange** their directions. 4 牛和 16 牛的力交换了方向，8 牛和 12 牛的力也交换了方向。

2 频

149 **exert** /ɪɡˈzɜːt/ *vt.* 运用，施加；竭力

1频

- 用 exert oneself 努力；尽力
- 例 Given that B is in equilibrium find, in terms of X, the normal component of the force **exerted** on B by the ground. 假设 B 处于平衡状态，用 X 表示，地面作用于 B 的向上的力的法向分量。

150 **expand** /ɪkˈspænd/ *v.* 展开，扩展

5频

- 反 contract *v.* 收缩
- 用 expand into （使）扩展，将……扩充成
- 例 In the *Pure Mathematics 2*, Chapter 7, you will learn how to **expand** these expressions for any real value of n. 在《纯数学 2》的第 7 章中，你将学习如何对 n 的任意实数值展开这些表达式。

151 **expansion** /ɪkˈspænʃn/ *n.* 膨胀，扩展，扩张

2频

- 用 rate of expansion 膨胀率
- 例 For this value of k, find the coefficient of x^2 in the **expansion**. 用已知的 k 值，求展开之后 x^2 的系数。

152 **expectation** /ˌekspekˈteɪʃn/ *n.* 期望值；预料，预期

3频

- 用 in expectation 期望着；意料之中
- 例 In this chapter we shall study continuous random variables as well as their **expectation** and variance. 本章我们将学习连续随机变量及其期望值和方差。

153 **expected** /ɪkˈspektɪd/ *adj.* 预期的，预料的

260频

- 同 anticipated, prospective
- 用 expected revenue 期望收益
- 例 Calculate the **expected** profit for the company. 计算公司的预期收益。

154 **experiment** /ɪkˈsperɪmənt/ *n.* 实验，尝试
　　　　　　　　　　　　　　　　　vi. 做实验

7频

- 用 experiment on sth. 对……进行实验
- 例 For a particular **experiment**, the temperature is initially 50℃,

and it is 45℃ one minute later. 在一场特定的实验中,最初温度是 50 摄氏度,一分钟后降到了 45 摄氏度。

155 **express** /ɪk'spres/ *vt.*(用符号等)表示,代表;表达
n. 快递服务

169频

- 用 express oneself 表达自己
- 例 **Express** the change in gravitational potential energy of the particle in terms of *x*. 用 *x* 表示质点重力势能的变化。

156 **expression** /ɪk'spreʃn/ *n.* 表达式,式;表示,表达

130频

- 用 mathematical expression 数学表达式
- 例 A highly skilled typist is comparing the abilities of two equation editing systems for the typing of complicated mathematical **expressions**. 一位技术娴熟的打字员正在比较两种方程式编辑系统对复杂数学表达式的编辑能力。

157 **extend** /ɪk'stend/ *v.* 扩展,扩大,延长

1频

- 同 expand
- 用 extend over sth. 涉及……;延伸至……
- 例 This allows you to check whether your proposed approach is likely to be fruitful or to work at all, and whether it can be **extended**. 它能使你检验出你的方案是成效显著还是仅仅行得通,以及是否可以进行扩展。

158 **external** /ɪk'stɜːnl/ *adj.* 外部的,外面的
n. 外观,外面

1频

- 反 internal *adj.* 内部的
- 用 external force 外力
- 例 The **external** surface area of the tank together with the area of the top the lid is 8 m². 罐子的表面积加上盖子顶部的面积为 8 平米。

F

159 **factorise** /ˈfæktəraɪz/ vt. 因数分解

9频

- 用 index factorise 指数分解
- 例 In this exercise you have to **factorise** a given number. 在此练习中，你要对所给数字作因数分解。

160 **ferry** /ˈferi/ n. 渡船
vt. 渡运，摆渡

3频

- 用 ferry passenger 运送旅客
- 例 The time taken, in minutes, by a **ferry** to cross a lake has a normal distribution with mean 85 and standard deviation 6.8. 渡湖时间呈正态分布，以分钟为单位，均值为 85，标准差为 6.8。

161 **fill** /fɪl/ v. 装满，填满
n. 填满的量

2频

- 用 fill the blank 填空
- 例 Packets of rice are **filled** by a machine and have weights which are normally distributed with mean 1.04 kg and standard deviation 0.017 kg. 每包米都是由机器装满的，重量呈正态分布，平均每包 1.04 公斤，标准差为 0.017 公斤。

162 **flight** /flaɪt/ n. 航班；飞行
v. 在空中飞行

2频

- 用 in flight 在飞行中；飞行状态
- 例 The probability that Julian gets a good night's sleep on a randomly chosen **flight** is 0.285. 朱利安在随机选择的航班上能睡个好觉的概率是 0.285。

163 fluid /ˈfluːɪd/ *n.* 液体，流体
adj. 流畅优美的

227频

- 用 correction fluid 修正液
- 例 For example, cubic equations are used in thermodynamics and fluid mechanics to model the pressure, volume or temperature behaviour of gases and **fluids**. 例如，热力学和流体力学中使用立方方程来模拟气体和流体的压力、体积或温度的行为。

164 force /fɔːs/ *n.* 力；力量；暴力
vt. 强迫

247频

- 用 the force of gravity 重力
- 例 The cyclist rides along a horizontal road against a total resistance **force** of 40 N. 这个骑自行车的人以克服 40 牛的总阻力沿水平道路骑行。

165 formation /fɔːˈmeɪʃn/ *n.* 结构；构造；组成

5频

- 同 structure
- 用 cloud formation 云层
- 例 The **formation** of the display is shown in the diagram. 显示器的结构如图所示。

166 frame /freɪm/ *n.* 支架，框架
vt. 做框；拟定

1频

- 用 frame rate 帧率，帧速率，帧频
- 例 Playground equipment consists of swings, climbing **frames** and play-houses. 游乐场设施包括秋千、攀爬架及游戏室。

167 friction /ˈfrɪkʃn/ *n.* 摩擦；摩擦力；冲突

101频

- 同 collision, collide (v.)
- 用 friction coefficient 摩擦系数
- 例 Calculate the coefficient of **friction** between the prism and the plane. 计算棱柱与平面之间的摩擦系数。

168 **frictional** /ˈfrɪkʃnl/ *adj.* 摩擦力的，由摩擦而生的

24 频

- 用 frictional resistance 摩擦阻力
- 例 The box moves up a line of greatest slope against a constant **frictional** force of 40 N. 在克服 40 牛的恒定摩擦力作用下，这个箱子沿着一条最陡的斜坡向上移动。

169 **fulfil** /fʊlˈfɪl/ *vt.* 完成；实现（愿望）；执行（任务）

1 频

- 回 complete, accomplish, carry out
- 用 fulfil oneself/sb. 实现自我；充分发挥潜能
- 例 What is the minimum height of tree required to **fulfil** this order? 完成此订单所需的最小树高是多少？

G

扫一扫
听本节音频

170 **goose** /guːs/ n. 鹅

8频

- goose liver 鹅肝
- A small farm has 5 ducks and 2 **geese**. 一个小农场有 5 只鸭子和两只鹅。
- geese

171 **gradually** /ˈgrædʒuəli/ adv. 逐渐地，渐渐地，逐步地

2频

- step by step
- gradually intensify 逐步加剧
- The value of *P* is **gradually** increased until the prism ceases to be in equilibrium. *P* 值逐渐增加，直到棱柱不再处于平衡状态。

172 **grant** /grɑːnt/ v.（合法）授予；赠予；承认
n.（政府、机构的）拨款

2频

- grant aid 给予帮助
- The authors and publishers acknowledge the following sources of copyright material and are grateful for the permissions **granted**. 作者和出版商承认以下版权材料的来源，并对被授予许可表示感谢。

173 **gravitational** /ˌgrævɪˈteɪʃənl/ adj. 引力的，重力引起的

5频

- gravitational field 引力场，重力场
- By Newton's third law, the Moon exerts a **gravitational** force of the same magnitude on the Earth. 根据牛顿第三定律，月球对地球施加了同样大小的引力。

174 **gravity** /ˈgrævəti/ n. 重力，引力；庄严

65 频

- 用 gravity field 重力场
- 例 *P* falls freely under **gravity** until it reaches the point *A* which is 1.25 m below *O*. 在重力的作用下，*P* 一直处于自由下落状态，直到到达位于 *O* 点上方 1.25 米处的 *A* 点。

175 **grid** /grɪd/ n. 网格；网状物；输电网

13 频

- 用 grid system 坐标制；方格网制；电力网
- 例 A coordinate **grid** is marked on a vertical wall. 坐标网格被标记在了一面墙上。

176 **gross** /grəʊs/ adj. 总的；毛的；令人恶心的
  adv. 全部
  n. 毛收入

1 频

- 同 aggregate (*adj.*)
- 用 gross weight 毛重
- 例 Ronnie obtained data about the **gross** domestic product (GDP) and the birth rate for 170 countries. 罗尼获得了 170 个国家的国内生产总值（GDP）和出生率的数据。

H

177　hang /hæŋ/ v. 悬挂；垂落
　　　　　 n. 下垂

42 频

- 用 hang about（在某处附近）等待，逗留，闲荡
- 例 The particles **hang** vertically. 质点垂直悬挂。

178　hence /hens/ adv. 从而，因此，由此

263 频

- 同 therefore, accordingly
- 用 from hence 由此处；从这里
- 例 Write down two equations involving p and q and **hence** find the coordinates of the possible positions of C. 写出两个包含 p 和 q 的方程，从而求出 C 可能位置的坐标。

179　highlighter /ˈhaɪlaɪtə(r)/ n. 荧光笔，亮光笔

96 频

- 用 use a highlighter 用荧光笔
- 例 The **highlighter** option includes custom colors so Bob can use different colors to highlight different sections. 可选自定义颜色的荧光笔，因此鲍勃可以使用不同的颜色来突出显示不同的内容。

180　histogram /ˈhɪstəɡræm/ n. 直方图，柱状图

21 频

- 用 frequency histogram 频率直方图
- 例 The following **histogram** represents the lengths of worms in a garden. 下面的直方图表示花园中蠕虫的长度。

40 | 国际课程数学核心词汇

181 **holder** /ˈhəʊldə(r)/ n. 持有者，拥有者；支托（或握持）……之物

239频
- 用 share holder 股东
- 例 A bank provides each account **holder** with a nine-digit card number that is arranged in three blocks. 银行为每个账户持有人提供一个 9 位数字的卡号，该卡号分 3 个区块排列。

182 **hollow** /ˈhɒləʊ/ adj. 中空的；凹陷的
n. 凹陷处
v. 挖

2频
- 近 empty (adj.), bare (adj.)
- 用 hollow pipe 空心管子
- 例 The diagram shows a **hollow** cone with base radius 12 cm and height 24 cm. 该图显示了一个底部半径为 12 厘米，高度为 24 厘米的空心圆锥。

183 **horizontal** /ˌhɒrɪˈzɒntl/ adj. 水平的，横的
n. 水平线，水平位置

376频
- 用 horizontal displacement 水平位移；水平变位
- 例 The board consists of vertical and **horizontal** lines. 该告示牌包含垂直和水平线。

I

184 identical /aɪˈdentɪkl/ *adj.* 完全同样的，相同的；同一的

28频

- 用 identical with sth. 与某物相同
- 例 Two rectangular boxes *A* and *B* are of **identical** size. *A* 和 *B* 两个矩形盒子大小相同。

185 identify /aɪˈdentɪfaɪ/ *vt.* 使相等；确认；视……为一样

1频

- 用 identify with the character of the play 代入到剧中人物的角色中
- 例 Prerequisite knowledge exercises **identify** prior learning that you need to have covered before starting the chapter. 必备知识训练相当于你学习本章之前需要掌握的内容。

186 identity /aɪˈdentəti/ *n.* 身份；同一性；特性

25频

- 用 a sense of identity 身份认同感
- 例 The **identity** of the infected person has yet to be confirmed. 被感染者的身份有待确认。

187 ignore /ɪɡˈnɔː(r)/ *vt.* 忽略，忽视，不予理会

1频

- 同 disregard
- 用 ignore pain 忽略痛苦
- 例 In practice this means you can safely **ignore** this constant. 实际上，这意味着你可以放心地忽略这个常数。

188 **illustrate** /ˈɪləstreɪt/ vt. (用示例、图画等)说明；加插图于；证明……存在

22频

- 同 demonstrate
- 用 illustrate A with B 用 B 给 A 加插图
- 例 Some examples of transformations are **illustrated** in this chapter. 本章中展示了一些转换示例。

189 **immediate** /ɪˈmiːdiət/ adj. 立即的，立刻的；目前的；直接的

2频

- 用 an immediate reaction/response 即时的反应/回应
- 例 She receives an **immediate** reply from a text message with probability 0.4, from an email with probability 0.15 and from social media with probability 0.6. 她收到一条及时回复的短信的概率为 0.4，收到电子邮件及时回复的概率为 0.15，收到来自社交媒体的即时回复概率为 0.6。

190 **inappropriate** /ˌɪnəˈprəʊpriət/ adj. 不合适的，不适当的

1频

- 反 appropriate adj. 合适的
- 用 be inappropriate to do sth. 不适合做某事
- 例 It would be **inappropriate** for me to comment. 由我评论并不合适。

191 **incline** /ɪnˈklaɪn/ vt. (使)倾斜；(使)倾向于

151频

- 用 incline A to/towards B 使 A 向 B 倾斜
- 例 A particle of mass 0.6 kg is placed on a rough plane which is **inclined** at an angle of 21° to the horizontal. 一个质量为 0.6 千克的质点被倾斜在一个与水平面成 21 度角的粗糙平面上。

192 **independent** /ˌɪndɪˈpendənt/ adj. 不相关的；独立的 n. 无党派议员

39频

- 用 independent variable 自变量，独立变量
- 例 Two events are said to be **independent** if either can occur without being affected by the occurrence of the other. 如果其中一个事件的发生不受另一个事件的影响，称两个事件是独立的。

193 indicate /ˈɪndɪkeɪt/ vt. 表明；象征；指出

3频

- 用 indicate by 用……指示
- 例 Her data **indicate** that 60% of the males and 70% of the females are wearing earphones at any given time. 她的数据表明，有 60% 的男性和 70% 的女性在任何给定时间内都佩戴着耳机。

194 inextensible /ˌɪnɪkˈstensɪb(ə)l/ adj. 不能扩展的，不能延伸的

90频

- 用 inextensible surface 不可展曲面
- 例 The beam is hinged at A to a fixed point on a vertical wall, and is held in equilibrium by a light **inextensible** rope. 横梁铰接在 A 点，垂直墙壁上的一个固定点上，由一根不能伸长的轻绳保持平衡。

195 infect /ɪnˈfekt/ vt. 传染（疾病）；腐蚀；使感染（某种感情）

8频

- 用 infect people with 2019-nCoV 传染新型冠状病毒给人们
- 例 A large field of area 4 km^2 is becoming **infected** with a soil disease. 一大片面积为 4 平方公里的土地正在受到一种土壤病害的侵害。

196 infinity /ɪnˈfɪnəti/ n. 无穷，无限；无穷大（的数）

39频

- 用 an infinity of stars 数不清的星星
- 例 Find the sum to **infinity** of this series. 求这个级数的无限相之和。

197 insert /ɪnˈsɜːt/ vt. 插入，嵌入；（在文章中）添加 n. 插页

25频

- 用 insert a coin into the slot 把硬币投入投币口
- 例 He **inserted** a small key into the lock. 他把一把小钥匙插进锁眼里。

198 **instant** /ˈɪnstənt/ *n.* 某一时刻；瞬间
adj. 立即的；即食的

96频

- 同 immediate (*adj.*)
- 用 instant message 即时通讯
- 例 Find the total time from the **instant** the rocket is fired until it returns to the ground. 求出从火箭点火到返回地面的总时长。

199 **instantaneous** /ˌɪnstənˈteɪniəs/ *adj.* 立即的；瞬间的

31频

- 同 instant, immediate
- 用 instantaneous action 瞬间动作
- 例 Find the distance between the two positions at which P is at **instantaneous** rest. 求 P 处于瞬时静止的两个位置间的距离。

200 **instead** /ɪnˈsted/ *adv.* 代替；反而；却

25频

- 用 instead of 代替；不是……而是……
- 例 Work you want to do, **instead** of just have to do. 选择你想做的工作，而不是为了工作而工作。

201 **instruction** /ɪnˈstrʌkʃn/ *n.* 操作指南；指示

416频

- 用 give sb. instructions to do sth. 命令某人做某事
- 例 You should follow the **instructions** on the front cover of the answer booklet. 你应该按照答案手册封面上的操作指南去做。

202 **internal** /ɪnˈtɜːnl/ *adj.* 内部的；体内的

3频

- 反 external *adj.* 外部的
- 用 internal bleeding 内出血
- 例 For the object as a whole, forces of interaction between the two parts are **internal** forces, and are not included in the equation. 对于物体整体而言，两部分相互作用的力是内力，不包含在等式中。

203 **intersection** /ˌɪntəˈsekʃn/ n. 交点，十字路口；交叉，相交

31频

- 用 road intersection 路口
- 例 Your sketch should indicate the coordinates of any **intersections** with the axes, but need not show the coordinates of any turning points. 你的草图应该体现出任何与坐标轴相交的点的坐标，但不需要体现出任何转折点的坐标。

204 **intersect** /ˌɪntəˈsekt/ v. 相交，交叉；贯穿

46频

- 用 be intersected by... 被……横穿
- 例 The graphs **intersect** at points A and B. 这些曲线在 A 点和 B 点相交。

205 **interval** /ˈɪntəvl/ n.（时间上的）间隔；幕间休息

55频

- 用 at regular intervals 每隔一定时间
- 例 Specify suitable axes and calculate the position of the ball at one second **intervals** for the first six seconds of its flight. 指定合适的坐标轴，计算球在飞行的前六秒中每隔一秒的位置。

206 **inverse** /ˌɪnˈvɜːs/ adj.（数量、位置）相反的，反向的

18频

- 用 inverse matrix 逆矩阵
- 例 The **inverse** of a function $f(x)$ is the function that undoes what $f(x)$ has done. 函数 $f(x)$ 的反函数是撤消 $f(x)$ 所做操作的函数。

207 **invert** /ɪnˈvɜːt/ v. 颠倒；(使)倒转；倒置 n. 转化

1频

- 用 invert sugar 转化糖
- 例 At time t seconds after the hole is cut, the paint in the cone is an **inverted** cone of depth h cm. 在开孔后的第 t 秒，圆锥体内的油漆形成了深度为 h 厘米的倒圆锥体。

208 invest /ɪnˈvest/ vt. 投资；投入（时间、精力等）；授予

- 同 grant
- 用 invest on sth. 投资于……
- 例 George wants to **invest** some of his monthly salary. 乔治想把自己月薪的一部分拿去投资。

2频

209 investigate /ɪnˈvestɪɡeɪt/ v. 调查，研究

- 用 investigate into sth. 对某事进行调查
- 例 A biologist is **investigating** the spread of a weed in a particular region. 生物学家正在调查这种杂草在特定地区的蔓延情况。

1频

210 invigilator /ɪnˈvɪdʒɪleɪtə(r)/ n. 监考人，监考老师；监视器

- 用 proctor invigilator 监考官
- 例 He was the **invigilator** of No. 2 Testroom. 他是第二考场的监考员。

25频

211 issue /ˈɪʃuː/ v. 发布；出版
n. 发行；重要的问题

- 用 economic issues 经济问题
- 例 Eight-digit mobile phone numbers **issued** by the Lemon Network all begin with 79. 柠檬网络发布的八位数手机号都是以 79 开头的。

124频

212 iterative /ˈɪt(ə)rətɪv/ adj. 迭代的；重复的，反复的
n. 反复体

- 用 cyclic iterative 循环迭代法
- 例 Use an **iterative** formula based on this rearrangement to determine the positive root correct to 2 decimal places. 使用以这种重新排列的迭代公式来确定正根（保留两位小数）。

70频

J

扫一扫
听本节音频

213 **junction** /'dʒʌŋkʃn/ n. （公路或铁路的）交叉路口，汇合处；连接

7频

- 同 intersection
- 用 junction station 枢纽站
- 例 Vehicles approaching a certain road **junction** from town A can either turn left, turn right or go straight on. 从 A 镇驶进某一路口的车辆可以左转、右转或直行。

214 **justification** /ˌdʒʌstɪfɪ'keɪʃn/ n. 正当理由；辩护

1频

- 用 in justification of sb./sth. 作为对某人/某事的解释（或辩护）
- 例 Determine, with **justification**, whether there is any instantaneous change in the acceleration of P when $t = 2$. 判断当 $t = 2$ 时，P 的加速度是否有瞬时变化。

215 **justify** /'dʒʌstɪfaɪ/ vt. 证明……正确；为……辩护

19频

- 用 justify amply 充分证明
- 例 Find the values of x at which the curve has a stationary point and determine the nature of each stationary point, **justifying** your answers. 找出曲线上有一个平稳点 x 的值，确定每个平稳点的性质，证明你的答案是正确的。

K

216 **kinetic** /kɪˈnetɪk/ *adj.* 运动的；运动引起的

19频

- 用 kinetic energy 动能
- 例 If this is the case, the **kinetic** energy at the top will also be zero. 如果是这样，顶部的动能也将为零。

L

217 leak /liːk/ v. 漏;泄露
n. 漏洞;泄露

2频

- 🌐 leak out 泄漏;泄出
- 📝 An oil pipeline under the sea is **leaking** oil and a circular patch of oil has formed on the surface of the sea. 海底的一条输油管道正在漏油,海面上出现了一小片圆形的油污。

218 limit /ˈlɪmɪt/ n. 极限;界限
vt. 限制;限量

27频

- 🌐 within the limits of sth. 在某事物的范围内
- 📝 The ring is in **limiting** equilibrium and on the point of sliding up the rod. 该环处于极限平衡状态,即将滑到杆上。

219 litre /ˈliːtə(r)/ n. 升

8频

- 🌐 per litre 每升
- 📝 It takes about one **litre** of water to produce one calorie from food crops. 粮食作物中产生一卡热量需要大约一升水。

220 loose /luːs/ adj. 不受约束的;宽松的;未固定的

1频

- 🌐 let sb./sth. loose 释放、放开某人或某物
- 📝 When the farmer's dog is let **loose**, it chases either the ducks with probability 3/5 or the geese with probability 2/5. 当农夫放开狗时,它追赶鸭子的概率是 3/5,追鹅的概率是 2/5。

221 lorry /ˈlɒri/ n. 卡车,货运汽车

47频

- 🌐 lorry crane 货车吊机;机动式起重吊车
- 📝 The goods will be carried by **lorry** to Dalian. 将用卡车把货物运往大连。

M

222 machine /məˈʃiːn/ n. 机器
vt. （用机器）制造，加工成型

3频

- 用 machine tool 机床
- 例 A **machine** saws planks of wood to a nominal length. 机器把厚木板锯成规定的长度。

223 magnitude /ˈmægnɪtjuːd/ n. 大小，量级；重要性

182频

- 同 account
- 用 earthquake magnitude 地震等级
- 例 Find the **magnitude** of the frictional force opposing the motion. 求出与运动相反的摩擦力的大小。

224 maintain /meɪnˈteɪn/ vt. 保持；维修；坚持（意见）

3频

- 用 maintain law and order 维持治安
- 例 This speed is **maintained** for a further 30 s. 这个速度又持续了 30 秒。

225 manufacture /ˌmænjuˈfæktʃə(r)/
n. 生产商，制造者

1频

- 用 manufacture exclusively 独家生产
- 例 A delivery of jackets is received from the **manufacturers** during the week. 一周内就可以从制造商那里收到一批夹克。

226 **measure** /ˈmeʒə(r)/ vt. 测量；判定
n. 措施；程度

- 同 degree (n.)
- 用 in full measure 最大程度的，最大限度地
- 例 Two different models are used to predict its height exactly 60 days after it was first **measured**. 用两种不同的模型预测它在第一次测量的 60 天后的高度。

227 **mechanics** /məˈkænɪks/ n. 力学；方法，手段

- 同 approach
- 用 quantum mechanics 量子力学
- 例 The seven chapters in this book cover the further **mechanics** required for the Paper 3 examination. 本书的七个章节涵盖了卷 3 所需的高数力学。

228 **medal** /ˈmedl/ n. 奖章，勋章
v. 获得奖章

- 用 gold medal 金牌
- 例 The number of Olympic **medals** won in the 2012 Olympic Games by the top 27 countries is shown below. 在 2012 年奥林匹克运动会中，排名前 27 位的国家所获奖牌的数量如下图所示。

229 **mess** /mes/ n. 肮脏；困境；大量

- 同 bunch
- 用 in a mess 杂乱不堪
- 例 The probability that the kitchen is left in a **mess** is 3/5. 厨房被弄得杂乱不堪的概率是 3/5。

230 **message** /ˈmesɪdʒ/ n. 信息，消息
vt. 向（某人）传送（电子信息）

- 用 get the message 领悟，理解
- 例 I left a **message** on your answering machine. 我在你的录音电话上留言了。

231 **million** /ˈmɪljən/ *n.* 一百万；大量

1频
- 用 one in a million 百里挑一，极稀有的人或事
- 例 There are 20 **million** people in country *X* and 8 **million** people in country *Y*. X 国有 2,000 万人，Y 国有 800 万人。

232 **minor** /ˈmaɪnə(r)/ *adj.* 轻微的
n. 辅修课程；未成年人

6频
- 用 minor injuries 轻伤
- 例 In the **minor** injuries clinic example, we chose to collect data on the number of patients arriving at the clinic in 30-minute intervals. 在轻伤诊所的例子中，我们选择收集了 30 分钟内到达诊所患者数量的数据。

233 **mixture** /ˈmɪkstʃə(r)/ *n.* 混合，混合物

1频
- 用 mixture ratio 混合比
- 例 Air is a **mixture** of gases. 空气是多种气体的混合物。

234 **model** /ˈmɒdl/ *vt.* 做成模型
n. 模型；设计

19频
- 用 business model 商业模式，经营模式
- 例 There are many situations in the real world that can be **modelled** as functions. 在现实世界中，有很多情况是可以建模为函数的。

235 **moment** /ˈməʊmənt/ *n.* 片刻；瞬间；准确的时刻

1频
- 同 instant, instantaneous (*adj.*)
- 用 for a moment 片刻，一会儿
- 例 He thought for a **moment** before replying. 他想了一下才回答。

236 motion /ˈməʊʃn/ n. 运动；动作；动议

- kinetic (adj.)
- motion graphics 动态图形
- Every object remains in a state of rest or of uniform **motion** in a straight line unless forces act on it to change that state. 每个物体都保持在一种静止或匀速直线运动的状态，除非外力作用于其上改变这种状态。

237 mutually /ˈmjuːtʃuəli/ adv. 相互地，彼此，共同地

- mutually beneficial 互利的；双赢的
- These three strategies are not **mutually** exclusive. 这三种策略并不是相互排斥的。

N

238 **navigation** /ˌnævɪˈgeɪʃn/ *n.* 航海；航行；导航

1频

- 用 radar navigation 雷达导航
- 例 Up till 500 years ago, our ancestors still led advancements in fields of metallurgy, economics, mathematics, nautical **navigation**, ceramics and silk. 直至500多年前，我们的祖先还在冶炼、经济、数学、航海、陶瓷、丝织等诸多方面引领着世界发展。

239 **negligible** /ˈneglɪdʒəbl/ *adj.* 微不足道的，不重要的

1频

- 同 minor
- 用 negligible difference 差别极小
- 例 The material from which the tank is made is of **negligible** thickness. 制造这个容器的材料的厚度可以忽略。

240 **network** /ˈnetwɜːk/ *n.* 网络；关系网；(互联)网络

1频

- 用 neural network 神经网络
- 例 There are 3 train apps, 6 social **network** apps and 4 games apps available. 一共有3款火车软件，6款社交软件和4款游戏软件。

O

241 observation /ˌɒbzəˈveɪʃn/ n. 观察，监察；评论

⊕ powers of observation 观察力
⑩ Anita made **observations** of the maximum temperature, t ℃, on 50 days. 安妮塔观察的 50 天内的最高温度为 t 摄氏度。

242 occasion /əˈkeɪʒn/ n. 某次；时机
vt. 使发生，造成

⊕ on occasion(s) 偶尔，偶然，有时
⑩ I've met him on several **occasions**. 我曾见过他几次。

243 occupy /ˈɒkjupaɪ/ vt. 使用，占用；忙着（做某事）

◉ take up 占据（时间，地方）
⊕ occupy a lot of space 占很多空间
⑩ The bed seemed to **occupy** most of the room. 床几乎占去了大半个房间。

244 operate /ˈɒpəreɪt/ vt. (被)使用，(使)运转
vi. 运转；经营

⊕ operate on sb./sth. 对某人动手术，对某物起作用
⑩ The proposal is to **operate** the scheme for a period of 24 months. 建议将该计划实施 24 个月。

245 opportunity /ˌɒpəˈtjuːnəti/ n. 时机，机会

⊕ take the opportunity of doing sth. 利用机会做某事
⑩ There was no **opportunity** for further discussion. 没有机会进行深入讨论了。

246 **orchard** /ˈɔːtʃəd/ *n.* 果园

1频
- 用 seed orchard 种子园，采种园
- 例 One hot summer day a fox was walking through an **orchard**. 炎炎夏日，狐狸路过果园。

247 **ordinary** /ˈɔːdnri/ *adj.* 普通的，平常的；平淡无奇的

6频
- 反 extraordinary *adj.* 非凡的，奇特的
- 用 out of the ordinary 不平常的；不寻常的
- 例 This word is seldom used on **ordinary** occasions. 这个词平时很少用。

248 **organism** /ˈɔːɡənɪzəm/ *n.* 有机生物体；人；有机组织

7频
- 用 marine organism 海洋生物
- 例 The sequence helps determine the traits of an **organism**. 该序列有助于确定一种生物体的特性。

249 **original** /əˈrɪdʒənl/ *adj.* 原来的，起初的；独特的

5频
- 用 original data 源数据
- 例 The researchers need the **original** data on the animal experiments. 研究者需要动物实验的原始数据。

250 **outcome** /ˈaʊtkʌm/ *n.* 结果，效果

2频
- 同 effect
- 用 the outcome of sth. 某事的结果
- 例 Draw a fully labelled tree diagram to show all the **outcomes**. 画一个完全标记的树形图来展示所有结果。

251 **outlier** /ˈaʊtlaɪə(r)/ *n.* （统计）异常值；（地质）外露层；局外人

3频
- 用 tectonic outlier 构造外露层
- 例 It is relatively unaffected by extreme values, also called **outliers**. 它相对不受极端值的影响，也被称为异常值。

252 **output** /ˈaʊtpʊt/ *n.* 输出量,产量;输出
　　　　　　　　　 vt. 输出

8频
- 反 input *n.* & *vt.* 输入
- 用 increase an output 增产
- 例 The power **output** is increased to 25 kW, the resistance to motion is unchanged. 输出功率增加到25千瓦,运动阻力不变。

253 **overestimate** /ˌəʊvərˈestɪmeɪt/ *vt.* 高估
　　　　　　　　　/ˌəʊvərˈestɪmət/ *n.* 过高的评价

2频
- 反 underestimate *vt.* 低估
- 用 overestimate oneself 自不量力
- 例 The scales may have underestimated or **overestimated** masses. 天平可能低估或高估了质量。

P

扫一扫
听本节音频

254 **packet** /ˈpækɪt/ *n.* (商品的)小包装纸袋;信息包,数据包

`19频`
- 用 postal packet 邮包
- 例 A shopper picks up a 2 kg **packet** of rice with the thumb and index finger of one hand. 顾客用一只手的拇指和食指提起2公斤重的一包大米。

255 **parallel** /ˈpærəlel/ *adj.* 平行的;对应的
　　　　n. 相似特征
　　　　vt. 与……相似

`113频`
- 同 corresponding (*adj.*)
- 用 parallel lines 平行线
- 例 The string is taut and **parallel** to a line of greatest slope of the plane. 细绳绷得很紧,平行于一条平面上斜率最大的直线。

256 **parcel** /ˈpɑːsl/ *n.* 包裹,小包;部分
　　　　vt. 包,裹好

`2频`
- 同 packet (*n.*)
- 用 part and parcel of 不可缺少的一部分
- 例 Three strings are knotted together at one end, and **parcels** of weights 5 N, 7 N and 9 N are attached to the other ends. 三根绳子在一端打结,重量分别为5牛、7牛和9牛的包裹绑在另一端。

257 **partial** /ˈpɑːʃl/ *adj.* 偏颇；部分的，不完全的

37频

- 用 be partial towards or to sb./sth. 偏袒或钟爱某人或某物
- 例 It has only **partial** derivatives for each variable. 这只有关于每个变量的偏导数。

258 **particle** /ˈpɑːtɪkl/ *n.* 质点；粒子；微粒

463频

- 用 dust particles 灰尘颗粒
- 例 A **particle** P of mass 0.8 kg is placed on a rough horizontal table. 一个质量为 0.8 千克的质点 P 被放置在一个粗糙的水平桌面上。

259 **particular** /pəˈtɪkjələ(r)/ *adj.* 特指的；特别的；讲究的 *n.* 详情

45频

- 用 in particular 尤其，特别
- 例 A farmer finds that 30% of his sheep are deficient in a **particular** mineral. 农民发现他养的羊有30%都缺乏某种矿物质。

260 **partner** /ˈpɑːtnə(r)/ *n.* 伙伴；合伙人；配偶 *vt.* 做搭档

1频

- 用 limited partner 有限合伙人，有限责任合伙人
- 例 Seven friends together with their respective **partners** all meet up for a meal. 7位朋友和他们各自的伙伴在一起聚餐。

261 **passenger** /ˈpæsɪndʒə(r)/ *n.* 乘客，旅客；闲散人员

18频

- 用 passenger transport 客运
- 例 A small aeroplane has 14 seats for **passengers**. 一架小型飞机有 14 个座椅。

262 **password** /ˈpɑːswɜːd/ *n.* 密码，口令；暗号

3频

- 用 password protection 密码保护
- 例 The **password** should be invisible. 密码应该是不可见的。

263 **peg** /peg/ *n.* 橛子，短桩；晾衣架子

13频

- 用 off the peg 成品的，现成的
- 例 A small company produces cylindrical wooden **pegs** for making garden chairs. 一家小公司生产圆柱木桩来制作花园椅。

264 **pepper** /ˈpepə(r)/ *n.* 甜椒，柿子椒；胡椒粉
          vt. 撒上胡椒粉

5频

- 用 pepper sb./sth. with sth. (以小物体) 频繁击打某人或某物
- 例 Another box contains 2 yellow peppers and 5 orange **peppers**. 另一个盒子里有 2 个黄色的辣椒和 5 个橙色的辣椒。

265 **period** /ˈpɪəriəd/ *n.* 一段时间；(人生或国家历史的) 阶段
         adj. 具有某个时代特征的

25频

- 用 peak periods 尖峰时刻
- 例 The four photographs above were taken over a **period** of time. 以上四张照片是在一段时间内拍摄的。

266 **permission** /pəˈmɪʃn/ *n.* 许可，批准；许可证

239频

- 用 without permission 未经许可
- 例 She took the car without **permission**. 她未经许可擅自使用汽车。

267 **permit** /pəˈmɪt/ *v.* 允许，准许
      /ˈpɜːmɪt/ *n.* 许可证；通行证

20频

- 用 residence permit 居留证
- 例 Throughout this question the use of a calculator is not **permitted**. 解答该题时，不允许使用计算器。

268 **petrol** /ˈpetrəl/ *n.* 汽油

7频

- 用 petrol engine 汽油发动机
- 例 A **petrol** station finds that its daily sales, in litres, are normally distributed with mean 4,520 and standard deviation 560. 一家

加油站发现它的日销售量（以升为单位）是正态分布的，平均值为 4,520，标准差为 560。

269 **plastic** /ˈplæstɪk/ *n.* 塑料
adj. 塑料的；可塑的；虚伪的

4频

- 用 plastic film 塑料薄膜；塑胶膜
- 例 Any material that, when stretched or compressed, does not return to its original form is said to be **plastic**. 任何材料，当被拉伸或压缩时，不能恢复到原来的形状，被称为塑料。

270 **plot** /plɒt/ *n.* 绘图；故事情节；阴谋
v. 绘图

2频

- 用 lose the plot 不知所措，迷惘
- 例 It is more common, however, for the data **plots** to lie on a curve. 然而，更常见的情况是在曲线上描点画图。

271 **possession** /pəˈzeʃn/ *n.* 私人物品；拥有

3频

- 用 in possession of sth. 拥有（或占有）某物
- 例 Each of these astronauts can take 3 personal **possessions** with him. 这些宇航员每人可以携带 3 件个人物品。

272 **possibility** /ˌpɒsəˈbɪləti/ *n.* 可能（性）；机会；潜力

1频

- 反 impossibility 不可能
- 用 a possibility of sth. ……的可能性
- 例 This Utopian dream is far beyond the range of **possibility**. 这种乌托邦式的梦想根本不可能实现。

273 **potential** /pəˈtenʃl/ *adj.* 潜在的，可能的
n. 潜力，可能性

16频

- 同 possibility (n.)
- 用 potential energy 势能
- 例 Find the elastic **potential** energy stored in the system. 求出系统中储存的弹性势能。

274 **power** /ˈpaʊə(r)/ *n.* 功率；控制力；能力
vt. 驱动

56 频

- 同 force (*vt.*)
- 用 electric power 电力；电功率
- 例 The **power** of the car's engine is a constant 36 kW. 汽车发动机的功率是恒定的 36 千瓦。

275 **precede** /prɪˈsiːd/ *v.* 在……之前发生（或出现）；先于

2 频

- 用 the preceding chapter 前一章
- 例 The earthquake was **preceded** by a loud roar and lasted 20 seconds. 地震发生之前有一声巨响，持续了 20 秒钟。

276 **predict** /prɪˈdɪkt/ *vt.* 预言；预告；预报

1 频

- 用 predict doing sth. 预测做某事
- 例 No one had enough foresight to **predict** the winner. 没人有足够的预见性可以预测准谁能获胜。

277 **presentation** /ˌpreznˈteɪʃn/ *n.* 解释，陈述，报告；出示；授予

244 频

- 用 graphical representation 图示，图解表示法
- 例 The professor will give a **presentation** on this matter tomorrow. 教授明天将就此事件进行解释。

278 **presenter** /prɪˈzentə(r)/ *n.*（广播、电视）节目主持人；演讲人；颁奖人

5 频

- 用 TV presenter 电视节目主持人
- 例 When Maria switches on the radio, the probability that it is set to station 3 and the **presenter** is male is 0.075. 玛丽亚打开收音机的瞬间，调到 3 台并且主持人是男性的概率是 0.075。

279 probability /ˌprɒbəˈbɪləti/ n. 概率；可能性；很可能发生的事儿

584频

- 同 possibility, potential
- 用 in all probability 很可能
- 例 You will study the mean of linear combinations of random variables in **Probability** and Statistics 2. 你将在《概率和统计学 2》中学到随机变量线性组合的均值。

280 production /prəˈdʌkʃn/ n. 生产；产量；(电影、戏剧或广播节目的)上映

1频

- 同 output
- 用 production process 生产流程
- 例 On a **production** line making cameras, the probability of a randomly chosen camera being substandard is 0.072. 在相机生产线上，随机选择相机的不合格概率是 0.072。

281 progression /prəˈɡreʃn/ n. 级数；连续；进程

151频

- 用 arithmetic progression 等差级数，等差数列
- 例 The first and second terms of a geometric **progression** are p and $2p$ respectively, where p is a positive constant. 等比级数的第一项和第二项分别为 p 和 $2p$，其中 p 为正常数。

282 properly /ˈprɒpəli/ adv. 正确地，适当地；得体地；实际上

4频

- 同 appropriately (adv.)
- 用 properly speaking 严格地说
- 例 This ensures the argument is **properly** rounded off. 这样可以确保函数的自变量是四舍五入的。

283 proportion /prəˈpɔːʃn/ n. 比例；份额；等比关系

12频

- 用 keep sth. in proportion 恰当地处事；看待事物恰如其分
- 例 It is found that the **proportions** choosing each brand are identical to those in the

smaller sample. 结果发现，每个品牌被选择的比例与小样本中的比例相同。

284 **proportional** /prəˈpɔːʃnl/ *adj.* 成比例的；相称的；均衡的

11频

- 🌐 inversely proportional 反比；成反比例
- 📝 Since the initialisation time is directly **proportional** to the size of the object the time is linear rather than constant. 由于初始化时间直接与对象的大小成比例，因此时间是线性的，而不是常量的。

285 **proportionality** /prəˌpɔːʃəˈnæləti/ *n.* 比例；均衡性；相称原则

1频

- 🌐 proportionality limit 比例极限，比例限度
- 📝 So from the **proportionality** relationship alone, we can tell the ratio of chances that you're in one state or another. 仅仅从比例关系，我们就可以知道你处于一个状态和另一个状态的机会比。

286 **proposal** /prəˈpəʊzl/ *n.* 提议，建议；求婚

1频

- 🌐 submit/consider/accept/reject a proposal 提交/考虑/接受/拒绝一项建议
- 📝 The **proposal** is still in discussion stage. 这个提案还处于讨论阶段。

287 **protect** /prəˈtekt/ *vt.* 保护；贸易保护；投保

239频

- 🌐 protect sb./sth. from/against sth. 保护……免受……
- 📝 These regulations were made to **protect** women. 这些规则是为了保护妇女而制定的。

288 **prove** /pruːv/ *v.* 证明；检验；证明是

38频

- 📖 justify
- 🌐 prove to be 证明是……
- 📝 You are asked to **prove** this in Exercise 6B Question 13. 请你在练习 6B 的第 13 题中证明这一点。

289 **provide** /prəˈvaɪd/ *vt.* 提供，给予；规定

1频

- 用 provide against sth. 预防某事，防备某事
- 例 Although both systems **provide** special facilities, they both have some difficulties in dealing with such expressions. 这两种系统虽然都提供了特殊的设施，但在处理这样的表达时都有一些困难。

290 **publisher** /ˈpʌblɪʃə(r)/ *n.* 出版人（或机构），发行人（或机构）

478频

- 近 issuer, bookmaker
- 用 art publisher 美术出版社
- 例 The **publishers** will be glad to make suitable arrangements with any copyright holders whom it has not been possible to contact. 出版商将很乐于为任何无法取得联系的版权持有人做出适当的安排。

291 **pulley** /ˈpʊli/ *n.* 滑轮，滑轮组；滑车

116频

- 用 pulley block 滑轮组
- 例 Another possibility is for the string to pass round a **pulley**, which can rotate on a fixed axis. 另一种可能是绳子绕过滑轮，滑轮可以在固定轴上旋转。

292 **pulse** /pʌls/ *n.* 脉搏；脉冲；强劲的音乐节拍

6频

- 用 pulse width 脉冲宽度
- 例 The doctor felt my **pulse**. 医生给我把了脉。

293 **puzzle** /ˈpʌzl/ *n.* 谜，智力游戏
　　　　　　　　　　vt. 迷惑，使迷惑

20频

- 用 puzzle over/about sth. 苦苦思索；仔细琢磨
- 例 The random variable X represents the time taken, in minutes, by a randomly chosen person to solve this type of **puzzle**. 随机变量 X 表示随机选择的人解决这类谜题所花费的时间，以分钟为单位。

Q

294 queue /kjuː/ n. 队列，行列
v. 排队等候

- 用 queue up 排队等候
- 例 A random sample of people **queuing** for a train ticket are asked how long they have been waiting in the **queue** before buying their ticket. 随机抽样排队买火车票的人，并询问他们买到火车票排了多久的队。

295 quiz /kwɪz/ n. 知识竞赛，智力游戏；小测验
vt. 盘问

- 用 quiz sb. about sb./sth. 盘问某人……
- 例 A television **quiz** show takes place every day. 电视智力竞赛节目每天都播出。

296 quotient /ˈkwəʊʃnt/ n. 商（除法所得的结果）

- 用 difference quotient 均差；差商
- 例 We already know how to divide a polynomial by a linear term and identify the **quotient** and any remainder. 我们已经知道如何用一个多项式除以一个线性项来确定商和任何余数。

R

297 **raise** /reɪz/ vt. 提升；举起；使自乘（若干次）
n. 提高

- 用 raise one's spirits 使某人振奋；使某人鼓起勇气 [4频]
- 例 A crane is used to **raise** a block of mass 50 kg vertically upwards at constant speed through a height of 3.5 m. 起重机可以将质量为 50 公斤的重物以恒定速度垂直向上提升至 3.5 米的高度。

298 **ramp** /ræmp/ n. 斜坡，坡道

- 用 access ramp 入口坡道 [11频]
- 例 The car then immediately descends another **ramp** of length 10 m inclined at 20° below the horizontal. 然后，（过山车）轿厢立即下降到另一个长度为 10 米、向下斜度为 20 度的坡道上。

299 **random** /ˈrændəm/ adj. 随机的，随意的
n. 随意，随机

- 用 at random 随机 [224频]
- 例 The information is processed in a **random** order. 信息是按照随机顺序处理的。

300 **rate** /reɪt/ n. 速度；比率；价格
vt. 评估

- 同 evaluate (v.) [2频]
- 用 exchange rate 汇率；兑换率
- 例 The cyclist continues to work at the same **rate** on the horizontal part ofd the road. 骑行者继续以同样的速度在水平路段骑行。

301 ratio /ˈreɪʃɪəʊ/ n. 比例，比率

26频

- 同 proportion, rate
- 用 utilisation ratio 利用率
- 例 Your expressions must contain at least two different trigonometric **ratios**. 表达式必须至少包含两个不同的三角比。

302 reaction /rɪˈækʃn/ n. 化学反应；回应；副作用

16频

- 用 reaction to sth. 对某事（物）的反应
- 例 In a certain chemical **reaction**, a compound A is formed from a compound B. 在某种化学反应中，化合物 A 由化合物 B 形成。

303 react /rɪˈækt/ vt. 发生化学变化；起反应；过敏

2频

- 用 react on 起作用于；对……有影响
- 例 In a certain chemical process a substance A **reacts** with another substance B. 在某种化学过程中，物质 A 与另一种物质 B 发生反应。

304 rearrange /ˌriːəˈreɪndʒ/ vt. 重新排列；重新安排；改变时间（或日期、地点）

2频

- 用 rearrange accounts 重置账户
- 例 The digits of the number 1,244,687 can be **rearranged** to give many different 7-digit numbers. 1,244,687 的 7 个数字可以重新排列得出许多不同的 7 位数字。

305 reasonable /ˈriːznəbl/ adj. 合理的；公平的；可接受的

239频

- 反 unreasonable adj. 不合理的
- 用 have a reasonable chance of doing sth. 有做某事的合理机会
- 例 This is a **reasonable** starting point but probably not accurate enough if we wanted a solution to this equation in the real world. 这是一个合理的起点，但如果我们想在现实世界中解决这个方程的话，可能不够精确。

306 rebound /rɪˈbaʊnd/ vi. 弹回，反弹；反作用于；回升

- 用 rebound in prices 价格回升
- 例 The highest point the ball reaches after **rebounding** is B. 球回弹后到达的最高点是 B。

307 recycle /ˌriːˈsaɪkl/ vt. 回收再利用；再次应用，重新使用（概念、方法、玩笑等）

- 用 recycle bin 回收站，资源回收筒
- 例 Two schemes are proposed for increasing the amount of household waste that is **recycled** each week. 为了增加每周可回收的生活垃圾的数量，现提出两个方案。

308 reduce /rɪˈdjuːs/ vt. 减少，缩小（尺寸、数量、价格等）；节食

- 同 decrease, diminish, lessen
- 用 reduce sth. from sth. to sth. 把……从……减少到……
- 例 After 6 pm all prices are **reduced** by 20%. 下午 6 点后，价格全部降低了 20%。

309 refer /rɪˈfɜː(r)/ vi. 涉及；参照；与……相关 vt. 使某人去某处

- 用 be referred to as... 被称为……
- 例 The questions asked in this example **refer** only to the upward motion of the ball. 本例中所问的问题仅指球的向上运动。

310 reference /ˈrefrəns/ n. 参考；提到 vt. 查阅；参考

- 用 for reference 以供参考；备案
- 例 Four books are randomly selected from a box containing 10 novels, 10 **reference** books and 5 dictionaries. 从一个装有 10 本小说、10 本参考书和 5 本字典的盒子里随机挑选出 4 本书。

311 **reflection** /rɪˈflekʃn/ *n.* 反射；映像；反映；思考

2频

- 用 be a bad reflection on sb./sth. 对某人/某事物的非议
- 例 As for any function and its inverse, the curves are **reflections** of each other in the line $y = x$. 对于任意函数及其反函数，都是互相关于 $y = x$ 对称的。

312 **refreshment** /rɪˈfreʃmənt/ *n.* 点心；提神；提神之事物

1频

- 扩 refreshed *adj.* 精神振奋的
- 用 in need of refreshment 需要提神
- 例 They queue up in a line for **refreshments**. 他们排队买点心。

313 **refuse** /rɪˈfjuːz/ *v.* 拒绝；拒绝做
n. 垃圾
adj. 无价值的

4频

- 用 a refuse dump 垃圾处理场
- 例 The sons **refuse** an offer to the beach with probability 0.65 and accept an offer to the park with probability 0.85. 儿子们拒绝去海滩提议的概率为 0.65，接受去公园提议的概率为 0.85。

314 **region** /ˈriːdʒən/ *n.* 地区，地方；行政区

216频

- 用 autonomous region 自治区
- 例 The shaded **region** is bounded by the curve. 阴影区域以曲线为界。

315 **reject** /rɪˈdʒekt/ *vt.* 拒绝接受；不录用
n. 次品

3频

- 同 refuse (*v.*)
- 用 reject ratio 废品率，不合格率
- 例 His sister **rejects** his invitation to the cinema. 他姐姐拒绝了他的电影邀请。

316 **relationship** /rɪˈleɪʃnʃɪp/ *n.* 关系，联系

7频

- 用 linear relationship 线性关系
- 例 One way to define a sequence is by thinking about the **relationship** between one term and the next. 定义序列的一种方法是考虑一个项和下一个项之间的关系。

317 **relative** /ˈrelətɪv/ *adj.* 相对的，相关联的；比较的
　　　　　　　　　　　　n. 亲戚

43频

- 用 relative standard deviation 相对标准偏差
- 例 This is a stretch of scale factor 2 in the x-direction: the distance **relative** to the y-axis has been doubled. 这是往 x 方向拉伸了两倍：相对于 y 轴来说，距离是两倍。

318 **release** /rɪˈliːs/ *vt.* 释放；发泄（情绪）
　　　　　　　　　　 n. 释放；发布

2频

- 同 issue (v.)
- 用 release rate 释放率
- 例 Particle A is **released** and the system begins to move. 质点 A 被释放，系统开始运动。

319 **remain** /rɪˈmeɪn/ *vi.* 保持不变；遗留
　　　　　　　　　　 n. 余物；遗迹

3频

- 用 the remains of ancient Greece 古希腊遗迹
- 例 If the ladder **remains** at rest (in equilibrium) then the resultant force is zero and the resultant moment is zero. 如果梯子保持静止（处于平衡状态），则合力为零，合力矩为零。

320 **remind** /rɪˈmaɪnd/ *vt.* 提醒，使想起

244频

- 扩 reminder *n.* 提醒
- 用 remind sb. to do sth. 提醒某人做某事
- 例 You are **reminded** of the need for clear presentation in your answers. 提醒你在作答时需要表达清楚。

321 **replace** /rɪˈpleɪs/ vt. 用……替换；代替；更换

2频

- 用 replace A with/by B 以 B 代替 A
- 例 Some people find it simpler not to substitute the numerical value 10 at first, but to **replace** it by a letter. 有些人发现，一开始不用数值 10 而用字母代替更容易。

322 **reply** /rɪˈplaɪ/ n. 回答
　　　　　　　　 vi. 回答，回复；回应

2频

- 同 react (vt.)
- 用 prompt reply 迅速答复
- 例 The question above was asked of a group of twelve 17-year-olds and each **reply** recorded as a number from 1 to 7, where 1 indicates 'agree strongly', and 7 indicates 'disagree strongly'. 上述问题是对一组 12 名 17 岁的青少年进行的调查，每项回答都被记录为 1 到 7 之间的一个数字，其中 1 表示"非常同意"，7 表示"非常不同意"。

323 **reproduce** /ˌriːprəˈdjuːs/ vt. 复制；再生产；繁育

239频

- 用 reproduce by 靠……繁殖
- 例 Past exam paper questions throughout are **reproduced** by permission of Cambridge Assessment International Education. 历年真题试卷题目全部由剑桥评估国际教育部许可转载。

324 **resist** /rɪˈzɪst/ vt. 阻挡；抵制；抑制

7频

- 用 resist doing sth. 抵制做某事
- 例 Hence find the distance AB, assuming there is no **resisting** force acting on the object. 因此，在假定物体上没有阻力的情况下，求出距离 AB。

325 **resistance** /rɪˈzɪstəns/ n. 阻力；反对，抵制

124频

- 用 electrical resistance 电阻
- 例 The only forces affecting the motion are the driving force and the **resistance**. 唯一影响运动的力是驱动力和阻力。

326 **respectively** /rɪˈspektɪvli/ adv. 分别；各自；依次为

193频

- 用 increased respectively 分别增加
- 例 The driving force of the car's engine is 2,500 N and the resistances to the car and trailer are 100 N and 150 N **respectively**. 汽车发动机驱动力为2,500牛，汽车和拖车的阻力分别为100牛和150牛。

327 **restriction** /rɪˈstrɪkʃn/ n. 限制规定；约束；制约因素

13频

- 同 limit
- 用 trade restriction 贸易管制
- 例 Since polar curves are defined with r ⩾ 0, we need to consider some **restrictions** for certain curves. 由于极坐标曲线定义为 r ⩾ 0，我们需要考虑到特定的曲线会有一些限制条件。

328 **resultant** /rɪˈzʌltənt/ adj. 因而发生的，因此而产生的

41频

- 用 resultant curve 合力曲线
- 例 This is usually called the **resultant** vector. 这通常称为合矢量。

329 **retake** /ˌriːˈteɪk/ vt. 补考，重修；收复（失地） n. 重拍（电影镜头）

2频

- 用 retake course 重修课程
- 例 Those students who fail are allowed to retake the test once, and the probability of any student passing the **retake** test is 0.65. 不及格的学生允许补考一次，补考通过的概率为0.65。

330 **revenue** /ˈrevənjuː/ n. 税收收入，财政收入；收益

2频

- 用 tax revenue 税收，赋税收入
- 例 The **revenue** per year is r million dollars when the rate of tax is x dollars per litre. 当税率为每升 x 美元时，每年的税收为 r 百万美元。

331 **reverse** /rɪˈvɜːs/ vt. 使反转；颠倒
n. 相反的情况
adj. 相反的

- 圊 inverse (n. & adj.), invert (n.) 2频
- 用 in reverse 相反
- 例 The particle hits a wall at the instant when $t = 60$, and **reverses** the direction of its motion. 当 $t = 60$ 时，质点在瞬间撞壁，并调转了运动方向。

332 **revolution** /ˌrevəˈluːʃn/ n. 旋转，绕轴旋转；革命；巨变

- 用 industrial revolution 工业革命，产业革命 5频
- 例 One complete **revolution** of the wheel takes 30 minutes. 一个车轮完整旋转一周需要 30 分钟。

333 **revolving** /rɪˈvɒlvɪŋ/ adj. 旋转的

- 用 revolving speed 转速 1频
- 例 You can visualise it **revolving** around the sun in a predictable orbital pattern. 你可以想象它按照预计轨道围绕太阳旋转。

334 **rigid** /ˈrɪdʒɪd/ adj. 坚硬的，不弯曲的；死板的

- 用 rigid arms 僵直的手臂 1频
- 例 The system of the car and trailer is modelled as two particles, connected by a light **rigid** horizontal rod. 汽车和拖车的系统被建模为两个质点，由一个轻而坚固的水平杆连接。

335 **rocket** /ˈrɒkɪt/ n. 火箭；烟花
vi. 快速增长 vt. 猛增

- 用 rocket launcher 火箭发射装置，火箭发射器 7频
- 例 After five seconds the **rocket** will be subject to one force only: its weight. 5 秒钟后，火箭将只受到一种力的作用：它的重量。

336 **rod** /rɒd/ *n.* 杆，竿，棒

26频

- 用 connecting rod 连杆
- 例 The diagram shows the cross-section of two cylindrical metal **rods** of radii x cm and j cm. 图为两个半径为 x 厘米和 j 厘米的圆柱形金属杆的横截面。

337 **roller** /ˈrəʊlə(r)/ *n.* 滚轴，滚柱；碾子

7频

- 用 roller coaster 过山车
- 例 The High **Roller** Ferris wheel in the USA has a diameter of 158.5 metres. 美国豪客摩天轮的直径为 158.5 米。

338 **root** /ruːt/ *n.* 根，方根；起源

86频

- 同 origin (*n.*)
- 用 square root 平方根
- 例 Verify by calculation that this **root** lies between 0.5 and 1. 通过计算验证此根位于 0.5 和 1 之间。

339 **rope** /rəʊp/ *n.* 绳索；围绳
　　　　　　　　　　 vt. 用绳子套；套紧

7频

- 用 steel rope 钢索，钢丝绳
- 例 The force accelerating the car is provided through the towing **rope**. 牵引绳为汽车加速助力。

340 **rough** /rʌf/ *adj.* 粗糙的；粗略的
　　　　　　　　　 n. 草图
　　　　　　　　　 vt. 画草图

90频

- 用 rough edges 瑕疵，美中不足之处
- 例 A particle of mass 5 kg is pulled, with constant speed, along a **rough** surface by a horizontal force of magnitude 45 N. 以 45 牛的水平力匀速拉动一个质量为 5 千克的质点经过一个粗糙的表面。

341 **row** /rəʊ/ n. 一行；(剧院、电影院等的)一排座位；
划船

vt. 排成一排

3频

- 用 in a row 接连，连续地
- 例 These 14 mugs are placed in a **row**. 这 14 个杯子被排成一排。

S

342 **salary** /ˈsæləri/ *n.* 薪金，薪水

⊕ a raise in salary 加薪

⊕ You are given that the median **salary** of the males is $24,000, the lower quartile is $22,600 and the upper quartile is $25,300. 假设男性的工资中位数是 24,000 美元，Q1 是 22,600 美元，Q3 是 25,300 美元。

6 频

343 **scalar** /ˈskeɪlə(r)/ *n.* 标量，纯量
adj. 无向量的

⊕ scalar multiplication 纯量乘法；标量乘法

⊕ You should know how to find the **scalar** product of two vectors and use it to find the angle between vectors. 你应该知道如何找到两个向量的点乘，并用它来找到向量之间的夹角。

23 频

344 **sector** /ˈsektə(r)/ *n.* 扇形；行业；地域，地带

⊕ sector length 扇面长度

⊕ The diagram shows a **sector** POQ of a circle of radius 10 cm and centre O. 该图为一个半径为 10 厘米、圆心为 O 的扇形 POQ。

41 频

345 **securely** /sɪˈkjʊəli/ *adv.* 安全地；牢固地；安心地

⊕ tie securely 扎紧

⊕ Tunneling can be utilised to **securely** communicate for almost any kind of service. 隧道技术可以用于几乎任何类型服务的安全通信。

244 频

346 **seek** /siːk/ *v.* 追寻；试图；询问

239频

- 用 seek to do good 试图行善
- 例 A force towards the centre is called a centripetal (centre-**seeking**) force. 朝向中心的力称为向心力（追心力）。

347 **segment** /ˈsegmənt/ *n.* 段，部分，片；弓形
vt. 划分

23频

- 同 part (*n.*)
- 用 line segment 线段
- 例 The diagram shows a metal plate made by removing a **segment** from a circle with centre *O* and radius 8 cm. 该图是一块金属板，它是从圆心为 *O*、半径为 8 厘米的圆上截取而得到的。

348 **separate** /ˈseprət/ *adj.* 不同的；单独的
/ˈsepəreɪt/ *vt.* （使）分开

2频

- 用 go your separate ways 分道扬镳，断绝往来
- 例 On a **separate** occasion, a random sample of *n* customers who went for a meal at the restaurant was taken. 在另一个场合，随机抽取了 *n* 名去餐馆吃饭的顾客。

349 **sequence** /ˈsiːkwəns/ *n.* 序列，顺序；连续
vt. 按顺序排列

16频

- 同 arrange
- 用 in sequence 依次，逐一
- 例 The next device in the **sequence** has 10 nails on four rows. 序列中的下一个装置有 10 个钉子，分布在 4 行上。

350 **serve** /sɜːv/ *vt.* 供应，提供；端上
n. 发球

5频

- 同 provide (*vt.*)
- 用 serve as 担任……，充当……，起……的作用

例 When Joanna cooks, the probability that the meal is **served** on time is x. 乔安娜做饭时能准时开饭的概率是 x。

351 **shade** /ʃeɪd/ vt. 画阴影，把……涂暗
n. 背阴，阴凉处

168频

- 用 shade into sth.（界线模糊地）渐变
- 例 Without using a calculator, find the area of the **shaded** region, giving your answer in an exact form. 不使用计算器，求阴影区域的面积，给出准确的答案。

352 **signal** /ˈsɪɡnəl/ n. 信号灯；标志；信号
adj. 出色的

6频

- 用 a signal feat 丰功伟绩
- 例 Now suppose that at a later time the train has to stop at a **signal**. 现在假设在以后的某个时间，火车在遇到信号灯时必须停车。

353 **significant** /sɪɡˈnɪfɪkənt/ adj. 有效的；重大的；有意义的

342频

- 用 significant figure 有效数字，有效数
- 例 Give your answers to 3 **significant** figures. 答案保留三位有效数字。

354 **silver** /ˈsɪlvə(r)/ adj. 银色的
n. 银色；银（币）
vt. 给……镀（或包）银

5频

- 用 silver medal 银质奖章；银牌奖
- 例 All the cars that were not red or **silver** in colour were grouped together as 'other'. 所有不是红色或银色的汽车都被归为"其他"之列。

355 **simultaneous** /ˌsɪmlˈteɪniəs/ *adj.* 同时发生（或进行）的；同步的

4频
- 回 instantaneous
- 串 simultaneous translation/interpreting 同声传译
- 例 The conference provides **simultaneous** translation in three languages. 会议提供三种语言的同声传译。

356 **skew** /skjuː/ *adj.* 斜的，歪的
vt. 偏离；使不公允

2频
- 回 deviate (v.)
- 串 skew angle 斜角
- 例 The photo on the wall is **skew**. 墙上的照片歪了。

357 **slack** /slæk/ *adj.* 松弛的；萧条的
n. （绳索的）松弛部分
vi. 怠慢

5频
- 回 loose (adj.)
- 串 slack off 偷懒；懈怠
- 例 *B* comes to rest without rebounding and the string becomes **slack**. B 在没有反弹的情况下静止了，绳子则变得松弛了。

358 **sledge** /sledʒ/ *n.* 雪橇
v. 乘雪橇

10频
- 串 sledge hockey 雪橇曲棍球，雪橇冰球
- 例 A runaway **sledge** of mass 10 kg travelling at 15 m s^{-1} reaches a horizontal snow field. 一辆质量为 10 公斤，以每秒 15 米速度行驶的失控雪橇到达水平雪地。

359 **slide** /slaɪd/ *v.* （使）滑行，滑动
n. （在冰上或光滑表面上）滑行；跌落

15频
- 串 slide block 滑块；滑架
- 例 A boy **slides** a box of mass 2 kg across a wooden floor. 一个男孩把一个 2 公斤重的箱子从木地板上滑过。

360 **slightly** /ˈslaɪtli/ *adv.* 稍微,略微;身材纤瘦的

1频

- 同 somewhat, slenderly
- 用 slightly damaged 轻微受损
- 例 The bead is **slightly** displaced from rest at A. 珠子在 A 点静止,然后稍微移动了一点位置。

361 **slope** /sləʊp/ *n.* 斜坡;倾斜;坡度
　　　　　　　　vi. 倾斜

94频

- 同 ramp (*n.*)
- 用 slope factor 斜率因子
- 例 A student on a geography field trip has collected data on the size of rocks found on a scree **slope**. 在一次地理实地考察中一名学生收集到了在一个碎石斜坡上发现的岩石大小的数据。

362 **smooth** /smuːð/ *adj.* 平滑的;平稳的;圆通的
　　　　　　　　vt. 使平滑

121频

- 用 smooth sth. away/out 消除(问题);克服(困难)
- 例 It is often difficult to fit a **smooth** curve through a set of plotted points. 通常很难通过一组绘制点来拟合平滑曲线。

363 **solar** /ˈsəʊlə(r)/ *adj.* 太阳能的,太阳的

2频

- 用 solar power/heating 太阳能动力/加热
- 例 In a certain country 12% of houses have **solar** heating. 在某个国家,12% 的家庭使用太阳能供暖。

364 **solid** /ˈsɒlɪd/ *adj.* 立体的;坚硬的;实心的
　　　　　　　　n. 固体

8频

- 同 rigid (*adj.*)
- 用 solid structure 立体结构
- 例 The horizontal base of a **solid** prism is an equilateral triangle of side x cm. 立体棱镜的水平底面是边长 x 厘米的等边三角形。

365 **species** /ˈspiːʃiːz/ n. 物种

9频

- 用 vulnerable species 濒危物种
- 例 Over the years, a biologist notes that a **species** of turtle lays on average 60 eggs in each nest. 多年来，一位生物学家注意到，有一种海龟每窝平均产 60 个蛋。

366 **specify** /ˈspesɪfaɪ/ vt. 明确规定；详述；详列

244频

- 用 specify vector 指定矢量
- 例 When defining a function, it is important to also **specify** its domain. 定义函数时，还必须写明定义域。

367 **speed** /spiːd/ n. 速度，速率；进度
vt. 快速运送

410频

- 近 rate (n.)
- 用 speed up 加速
- 例 A manager asks each of these workers to assemble a phone at their normal working **speed**. 经理要求工人们以正常的工作速度来组装电话。

368 **sphere** /sfɪə(r)/ n. 球体；领域；(包围地球等的大气的) 层

1频

- 近 domain
- 用 a perfect sphere 完美的球体
- 例 You may assume that this happens before P comes into contact with the **sphere** again. 你可以假设这发生在 P 再次与球体接触之前。

369 **spherical** /ˈsferɪkl/ adj. 球形的，球状的

2频

- 用 spherical geometry 球面几何学
- 例 The volume of a **spherical** balloon is increasing at a constant rate of 50 cm^3 per second. 球形气球的体积以每秒 50 立方厘米的恒定速率增加。

370 **spinner** /ˈspɪnə(r)/ n. 纺纱工人；纺纱机

35 频

- 用 wheel spinner 转向盘
- 例 A **spinner** is the person who makes thread by spinning. 纺纱工就是纺织制线的人。

371 **spin** /spɪn/ v. (使)快速旋转；纺(纱)
n. 旋转；眩晕

1 频

- 近 revolution (n.), revolving (adj.)
- 用 spin cotton into thread 把棉纺成纱
- 例 Axel decides to **spin** the wheel 400 times. 阿克塞尔决定让轮子旋转 400 圈。

372 **spread** /spred/ v. (使)蔓延，扩散；展开
n. 传播，蔓延

3 频

- 近 expand (v.)
- 用 spread like wildfire 像野火般蔓延；迅速传开
- 例 A biologist is investigating the **spread** of a weed in a particular region. 生物学家正在调查一种杂草在特定地区蔓延的情况。

373 **sprinter** /ˈsprɪntə(r)/ n. 短跑选手

7 频

- 用 elite sprinters 优秀短跑运动员
- 例 A **sprinter** runs a race of 400 m. 短跑运动员参加 400 米赛跑。

374 **staple** /ˈsteɪpl/ n. 订书钉
adj. 主要的，基本的
vt. 用订书钉装订

227 频

- 用 staple remover 起钉机，起钉器
- 例 Do not use **staples**, paper clips, highlighters, glue or correction fluid. 请勿使用订书钉、回形针、荧光笔、胶水或修正液。

375 **stem** /stem/ n. （植物的）茎，梗；词干
v. 阻止

21频

- 用 stem from 起源于，来自，来自于
- 例 The **stem**-and-leaf diagram shows the data. 茎叶图显示了数据。

376 **stick** /stɪk/ n. 条状物；枝条
vt. 粘住；坚持

1频

- 用 stick at sth. 坚持不懈地做（某事），锲而不舍
- 例 Swati measured the lengths, x cm, of 18 **stick** insects and found that $\Sigma x^2 = 967$. 斯瓦蒂测量了18种长度为 x 厘米的竹节虫，发现 x^2 的和等于967。

377 **straight** /streɪt/ adj. 直的
adv. 成直线地
n. 直道

247频

- 用 get sth. straight 明确某事；把某事弄清楚
- 例 The particle model is adequate here: the tray travels in a **straight** line in the direction of the applied force. 这里的质点模型是足够的：托盘沿着作用力的方向直线运动。

378 **straw** /strɔː/ n. （喝饮料用的）吸管；麦秆，稻草

7频

- 用 a straw hat 草帽
- 例 Plastic drinking **straws** are manufactured to fit into drinks cartons which have a hole in the top. 塑料吸管是用来插入顶部有孔的软包装饮料盒里的。

379 **string** /strɪŋ/ n. 细绳；一串
vi. 扎
adj. 线的

290频

- 同 rope (n. & v.)
- 用 a string of 一系列，一串
- 例 They are connected by a light **string** of length 4 m. 它们由一根4米长的细绳连接。

380 **subsequent** /'sʌbsɪkwənt/ adj. 随后的，后来的，之后的

11频

- ⊕ subsequent functions 后续函数
- 例 It does not reach the pulley in the **subsequent** motion. 它在随后的运动中无法到达滑轮。

381 **subsequently** /'sʌbsɪkwəntli/ adv. 随后，后来，接着

8频

- ⊕ release subsequently 随后释放
- 例 The car **subsequently** passes through the point C. 汽车随后通过 C 点。

382 **subsidiary** /səb'sɪdiəri/ adj. 辅助的；附带的 n. 子公司

183频

- ⊕ subsidiary subject 辅修课
- 例 The marketing department has always played a **subsidiary** role to the sales department. 市场部一直都在辅助销售部。

383 **substance** /'sʌbstəns/ n. 物质；物品；主旨

11频

- ⊕ the susbtance of one's lecture 某人演讲的主旨
- 例 A **substance**, X, is decaying such that the rate of change of the mass, x, is proportional to four times its mass. 一种物质 X 正在衰变，以至于质量变化率 x 与其质量的四倍成正比。

384 **substandard** /ˌsʌb'stændəd/ adj. 不合格的；不达标的

2频

- ⊕ substandard goods 劣等品，处理品
- 例 On a production line making cameras, the probability of a randomly chosen camera being **substandard** is 0.072. 在摄像机生产线上，随机选择的摄像机不合格的概率为 0.072。

385 **substitution** /ˌsʌbstɪ'tjuːʃn/ *n.* 代替；代替物；置换

35频

- 同 replacement (*n.*)
- 用 substitution method 代入法；替换法
- 例 A **substitution** method is often, a quicker alternative. 替代法通常是一种更快的解决办法。

386 **subtract** /səb'trækt/ *vt.* 减，减去

1频

- 反 add *v.* 加
- 用 subtract sth. from sth. 从……减……
- 例 Each module was an arithmetical command such as add, **subtract**, multiply, cosine, sine. 每一个组件都是一种算数指令，诸如加、减、乘、余弦、正弦。

387 **suddenly** /'sʌdənli/ *adv.* 突然，猛地，骤然

2频

- 同 abruptly
- 例 It all happened so **suddenly**. 一切都来得那么突然。

388 **Sudoku** /suˈdəʊkuː/ *n.* 数独，九宫格游戏

4频

- 用 Sudoku master 数独大师，数独达人
- 例 The probability that Sue completes a **Sudoku** puzzle correctly is 0.75. 苏正确完成数独游戏的概率是 0.75。

389 **sufficient** /səˈfɪʃnt/ *adj.* 足够的，充足的

1频

- 用 sufficient condition 充分条件
- 例 These reasons are not **sufficient** to justify the ban. 这些理由不足以证明实施禁令有理。

390 **summary** /'sʌməri/ *n.* 总结；概括
adj. 概括的；从速从简的

4频

- 用 in summary 总之，概括起来
- 例 A **summary** of 30 values of x gave the following information. 对 x 的 30 个值的总结给出了以下信息。

391 surd /sɜːd/ *n.* 不尽根，无理数
adj. 不尽根的

1 频

- ⊕ binomial surd 二项不尽根
- ⑳ Find the median value, giving your answer in **surd** form. 找到中间值，用不尽根形式给出答案。

392 surface /ˈsɜːfɪs/ *n.* 表面；水面；操作台
vi. 露面

68 频

- ⊕ on the surface 表面上，外表上
- ⑳ Another example is that a stone is sent sliding across the frozen **surface** of a lake. 另一个例子是当一块石头滑过冰冻的湖面。

393 surround /səˈraʊnd/ *vt.* 环绕；包围
n. 边缘；周围

1 频

- ⊕ surround sound 环绕立体声
- ⑳ The ball strikes the horizontal ground which **surrounds** the building at a point A. 球在 A 点击中了围绕建筑物的水平地面。

394 survey /ˈsɜːveɪ/ *n.* 调查；测量，测绘
/səˈveɪ/ *vt.* 查看

10 频

- ⊜ investigate (*v.*)
- ⊕ survey data 测量数据，测量资料
- ⑳ In a **survey**, the percentage of meat in a certain type of takeaway meal was found. 在一项调查中，人们发现了某种外卖食品中含肉的比例。

395 switch /swɪtʃ/ *vt.* (使)改变，转变
n. (电路的)开关，闸

3 频

- ⊕ switch on 接通，开启，合闸
- ⑳ A car travels down a hill which is inclined at 6° to the horizontal, with its engine **switched** off. 汽车在发动机熄火的情况下，沿着与水平面成 6 度角的山坡下行。

396 **symbol** /'sɪmbl/ *n.* 符号；象征

1频

- 同 signal
- 用 symbol for sth. 代号，记号
- 例 We shall use the **symbols** explained in the key point. 我们将使用要点中解释过的符号。

397 **symmetry** /'sɪmətri/ *n.* 对称；相似，相等

1频

- 用 axial symmetry 轴对称，轴对称性
- 例 A snowflake has the incredible beauty and **summetry**. 雪花有令人难以置信的美丽和对称。

398 **syndicate** /'sɪndɪkət/ *n.* 财团；企业联合组织；私人联合会

239频

- 用 loan syndicate 贷款财团
- 例 But Greece and Ireland may not be treated so kindly, which is why their recent issues have been through a **syndicate**. 但是希腊和爱尔兰或许无法获得如此优待，这就是为什么两国最近的国债发行都是通过财团的原因。

T

399 **tail** /teɪl/ *n.* 硬币反面；尾部，尾巴
　　　　　　　vt. 跟踪，尾随

3频

- ⊕ the long tail 长尾理论；长尾巴
- ⓔ Find the probability that there are more heads than **tails** when three coins are tossed. 算出抛掷 3 枚硬币时正面多于背面的概率。

400 **temperature** /ˈtemprətʃə(r)/ *n.* 温度，气温；体温

7频

- ⊕ raise/lower the temperature 升 / 降温；增加 / 减少热烈程度
- ⓔ The probability of the minimum **temperature** being above 6℃ on any winter day is 0.0735. 冬天任意一天最低气温高于 6 摄氏度的概率为 0.0735。

401 **tension** /ˈtenʃn/ *n.* 张力；紧张
　　　　　　　vt. （使金属线、帆等）拉紧

90频

- ⊕ international tensions 国际紧张局势
- ⓔ The string is at right angles to BC and the **tension** in the string is T N. 细绳与 BC 成直角，细绳的张力为 T 牛。

402 **theorem** /ˈθɪərəm/ *n.* 定理，原理

2频

- ⊕ Pythagoras' theorem 勾股定理；毕达哥拉斯定理
- ⓔ They form the basis of the central limit **theorem**. 它们构成了中心极限定理的基础。

403 **thickness** /ˈθɪknəs/ *n.* 厚度；厚；层

1频

- 回 aggregate thickness 总厚度
- 例 A paper mill produces sheets of paper, each of a constant **thickness**. 造纸厂生产纸张，每张纸的厚度都是一样的。

404 **thread** /θred/ *vt.* 穿成串；穿过
n. (棉、毛、丝等的)线

16频

- 回 cable (*n.*), string (*n.*)
- 用 thread A through B 将 A 穿过 B
- 例 A small ring *P* of mass 0.03 kg is **threaded** on a rough vertical rod. 一个质量为 0.03 千克的小环 *P* 被串在粗糙的立柱上。

405 **throughout** /θruːˈaʊt/ *prep.* 自始至终；遍及
adv. 全部

22频

- 回 gross (*adv.*)
- 用 uniform throughout 均匀连续分布
- 例 **Throughout** the series, the emphasis is on understanding the mathematics as well as routine calculations. 在整个系列中，重点是理解数学和常规计算。

406 **throw** /θrəʊ/ *vt.* 扔，投，掷
n. 掷(骰子)

19频

- 用 throw over 抛弃，遗弃
- 例 A dart is randomly **thrown** at the board, so that it sticks within its perimeter. 一个飞镖被随意地投向靶盘，结果粘在了靶盘的边缘上。

407 **toss** /tɒs/ *vt.* 掷硬币决定；使摇动

2频

- 回 flip
- 用 toss sb. sth. 把某物扔给某人
- 例 Four unbiased coins are **tossed** and the number of heads (*X*) is noted. 投掷四枚没有动过手脚的硬币，并记下头像面 (*X*) 的数量。

408 **trace** /treɪs/ *vt.* 追踪，找到；追究
n. 痕迹

239频

- 用 all traces of sth. ……的所有痕迹（或踪迹、遗迹）
- 例 A locus is a path **traced** out by a point as it moves following a particular rule. 轨迹是一个点沿着特定规则移动时追踪的路径。

409 **trapezium** /trəˈpiːziəm/ *n.* 梯形

19频

- 用 isosceles trapezium 等腰梯形
- 例 The shaded area consists of a **trapezium** and a rectangle. 阴影区域是由一个梯形和一个矩形组成。

410 **treasurer** /ˈtreʒərə(r)/ *n.* 会计，出纳，财务主管

2频

- 同 accountancy
- 用 assistant treasurer 副财务主管
- 例 For small firms, the **treasurer** is likely to be the only financial executive. 对于规模较小的公司，会计很可能是公司财务的唯一负责人。

U

411 underestimate /ˌʌndərˈestɪmət/ n. 低估，轻视
/ˌʌndərˈestɪmeɪt/ v. 低估，轻视

- 反 overestimate n. & v. 高估
- 用 seriously underestimate sth. 严重地低估某事
- 例 However, small errors are more likely than large errors and our measurements are usually just as likely to be underestimates as **overestimates**. 然而，小误差比大误差发生的可能性更大，所以我们的测量结果既可能高估也可能低估。

412 undertake /ˌʌndəˈteɪk/ vt. 承担，从事；承诺

- 用 undertake a task 承担一项任务
- 例 University professors both teach and **undertake** research. 大学教授既要教学又要从事研究工作。

413 underweight /ˌʌndəˈweɪt/ adj. 重量不足的

- 用 modest underweight 轻微减持
- 例 Crates of tea should contain 200 kg, but it is known that 1 out of 45 crates, on average, is **underweight**. 一箱茶叶应该重200公斤，但据了解，平均45箱茶叶中会有1箱重量不足。

414 uniformly /ˈjuːnɪfɔːmli/ adv. 一致地

- 用 uniformly consistency 一致相合性，均匀相合性
- 例 The driver speeds up **uniformly** over the next 30 s to reach a speed of 30 m s^{-1}. 司机在接下来的30秒内均匀加速，达到30米每秒的速度。

415 **unless** /ənˈles/ conj. 除非
prep. 除……之外

244频

- 用 unless and until 直到……才
- 例 This is the model you should use, **unless** you are told otherwise. 这是你应该使用的模型，除非别人告诉你不可以。

416 **unsimplified** /ˌʌnˈsɪmplɪfaɪd/ adj. 未简化的

1频

- 用 unsimplified Chinese 繁体中文
- 例 **Unsimplified** Chinese characters are not used in most parts of China any more. 繁体字已经不在中国大部分地区使用了。

417 **unwittingly** /ʌnˈwɪtɪŋli/ adv. 糊里糊涂地，茫然，不知不觉地

239频

- 用 almost unwittingly 几乎在不经意间
- 例 **Unwittingly**, they have been influenced by a completely irrelevant number. 不知不觉中，一个毫不相关的数字影响到了他们。

418 **uppermost** /ˈʌpəməʊst/ adj. 最高的；最关键的
adv. 处于最高位置

1频

- 同 highest, supreme
- 用 the uppermost floor 最高层
- 例 The force on the **uppermost** sphere is now removed. 最上面球体上的力现在被移除了。

419 **upright** /ˈʌpraɪt/ adj. 正直的；垂直的，直立的
n. 垂直

1频

- 用 upright position 正浮位置，直坐式
- 例 Take two books, one heavier than the other, and stand each **upright** on a table. 拿两本书，一本要比另一本重，且两本都立在桌子上。

V

420 **variable** /ˈveəriəbl/ n. 变量；可变情况
adj. 多变的；易变的

78频

- 用 random variable 随机变量
- 例 The following table shows the probability distribution for the random **variable** X. 下表显示了随机变量 X 的概率分布。

421 **various** /ˈveəriəs/ adj. 各种各样的；多姿多彩的

1频

- 用 various times 不同的时期
- 例 A bowl of mass 500 grams is placed on a table, which is tilted at **various** angles to the horizontal. 一个 500 克重的碗放在桌子上，桌子以不同的角度向水平方向倾斜。

422 **vehicle** /ˈviːəkl/ n. 车辆；手段，工具

15频

- 近 approach, mechanics
- 用 vehicle maintenance 汽车维护
- 例 The following table shows the front tyre pressure, in psi, of five 4-wheeled **vehicles**, A to E. 下表显示了五辆四轮车辆 A 到 E 的前轮胎压力，单位是 psi。

423 **velocity** /vəˈlɒsəti/ n. 速度；高速

145频

- 近 rate, speed
- 用 velocity distribution 速度分布
- 例 As the object follows its path the horizontal component of **velocity** is unchanged. 当物体沿着它的路径运动时，速度的水平分量不变。

424 **vertex** /ˈvɜːteks/ n. 顶点，(三角形或锥形的)角顶；至高点

6频

- 同 uppermost (adj.)
- 用 vertex angle 顶角
- 例 A quarter circle, of radius 10 cm, is drawn with the **vertex** of the square as centre. 以正方形顶点为中心画一个半径为10厘米的四分之一圆。

425 **vowel** /ˈvaʊəl/ n. 元音，元音字母

10频

- 用 long vowel 长元音
- 例 Each language has a different **vowel** system. 每种语言都有不同的元音系统。

W

扫一扫
听本节音频

426 **whisker** /ˈwɪskə(r)/ *n.* (猫、鼠等的)须；络腮胡子

18频

- 用 whisker plot 须状图盒
- 例 The numbers of golf shots are summarised in a box-and-**whisker** diagram. 高尔夫球的击球次数用盒须图汇总。

427 **wire** /ˈwaɪə(r)/ *n.* 金属丝；电线
vt. 用导线给(建筑物、设备等)接通电源

12频

- 用 wire rope 钢丝索
- 例 A piece of **wire** of length 24 cm is bent to form the perimeter of a sector of a circle of radius r cm. 将一段长度为24厘米的金属丝弯曲，形成一个半径为 r 厘米的圆的扇形区域的周长。

428 **wrap** /ræp/ *vt.* 包装；用……包裹

5频

- 同 surround
- 用 be wrapped up in sth. 专心致志于某事
- 例 The maker of a certain brand of chocolate sells boxes of individually **wrapped** chocolates. 某品牌巧克力的生产商出售单独包装的盒装巧克力。

第二部分
高频专业词汇

第一章 8~10 年级高频专业词汇 / 100

第一节 Pure Mathematics 纯数 / 100

第二节 Statistics 统计 / 133

第二章 11~12 年级高频专业词汇 / 140

第一节 Pure Mathematics 纯数 / 140

第二节 Statistics 统计 / 169

第三节 Mechanics 力学 / 200

8~10年级高频专业词汇

第一节
Pure Mathematics 纯数

第一小节　Numbers 数字

扫一扫
听本节音频

001　arithmetic /əˈrɪθmətɪk/　　　　　　　　　　*n.* 算术

- 🇬🇧 The basic arithmetic operations are addition, subtraction, multiplication and division.
- 🇨🇳 基本的算术运算是加、减、乘、除。
- 拓 arithmetic sequence 等差数列
  - Each term in the progression differs from the term before by a constant. For example 1, 3, 5, 7, 9, 11 etc. is an arithmetic sequence.
  - 等差数列即数列中的每一项与它的前一项的差等于同一个常数的一种数列。例如1、3、5、7、9、11。

002　decimal /ˈdesɪml/　　　　　　　　　　　　　*n.* 小数

- 🇬🇧 a fraction (= a number less than one) that is shown as a dot or point followed by the number of tenths, hundredths, etc
- 🇨🇳 小数即一个小于1的分数用一个圆点（即小数点）后面跟着十分位、百分位等数字表示出来。
- 拓 decimal places 小数位
  - The position of a number after a decimal point.
  - 小数位是一个数字在小数点后的位置。

003　fraction /ˈfrækʃn/　　　　　　　　　　　　*n.* 分数

- 🇬🇧 a division of a number, for example 5/8
- 🇨🇳 分数是一个数的除法，例如 5/8。

- 扩 improper fraction 假分数
  - a fraction in which the top number is greater than the bottom number, for example 7/6
  - 假分数是分子大于分母的分数，例如 7/6。

  proper fraction 真分数
  - a fraction that is less than one, with the bottom number greater than the top number, for example 1/4
  - 真分数是小于 1 且分母大于分子的分数，例如 1/4。

004 **add** /æd/   vi. 加 vt. 计算……的总和 n. 加法

- 基 to put numbers or amounts together to get a total
- 释 加即把数、量加在一起得到总数。
- 同 plus (prep.)
- 扩 addition n. 加法
  - The process of adding two or more numbers together to find their total.
  - 加法即把两个或两个以上的数字加起来求和的计算过程。

005 **subtract** /səbˈtrækt/   vt. 减

- 基 to take a number or an amount away from another number or amount
- 释 减即从一个数、量中去掉另一个数、量。
- 同 minus
- 扩 subtraction n. 减法
  - the process of subtracting two or more numbers together to find their total
  - 减法即把两个或两个以上的数字相减的计算过程。

006 **multiply** /ˈmʌltɪplaɪ/   v. 乘

- 基 to add a number to itself a particular number of times
- 释 乘即把同一个数字按特定的次数相加。
- 同 times
- 扩 multiplication n. 乘法
  - the process of multiplying of two or more numbers
  - 乘法即两个或多个数相乘的过程。

007 **divide** /dɪˈvaɪd/   v. 除，除以

🅔 to find out how many times one number is contained in another

㊣ 除即计算出一个数字是另一个数字的几倍。

㊕ division *n.* 除法
- the process of dividing one number by another
- 除法即一个数除以另一个数的过程。

008 **numerator** /ˈnjuːməreɪtə(r)/   *n.* 分子

🅔 the number above the line in a fraction, for example 3 in the fraction 3/4

㊣ 分子是分数线上的数字，例如分数 3/4 中的 3。

㊕ denominator *n.* 分母

009 **denominator** /dɪˈnɒmɪneɪtə(r)/   *n.* 分母

🅔 the number below the line in a fraction showing how many parts the whole is divided into, for example 4 in 3/4

㊣ 分母是分数线下的数字，表示整体被分成多少部分，例如 3/4 中的 4。

㊕ numerator *n.* 分子

010 **integer** /ˈɪntɪdʒə(r)/   *n.* 整数

🅔 a whole number, such as 3 or 4 but not 3.5

㊣ 整数是一个完整的数字，例如 3 或 4 是整数，但 3.5 不是整数。

011 **prime** /praɪm/ **number**   质数，素数

🅔 a number that can be divided exactly only by itself and 1, for example 7, 17 and 41, etc

㊣ 质数是一个只能被自身和 1 整除的数字，例如 7、17、41 等。

012 **natural** /ˈnætʃrəl/ **number**   自然数

🅔 a positive whole number such as 1, 2, or 3, and sometimes also zero

㊣ 自然数是一个正整数，例如 1、2、3，有时也包括 0。

013 **odd** /ɒd/ **number** 奇数

- **E** the number that cannot be divided exactly by the number two
- **释** 奇数是不能被数字 2 整除的数。

014 **even** /ˈiːvn/ **number** 偶数

- **E** the number that can be divided exactly by two
- **释** 偶数是能被 2 整除的数。

015 **square** /skweə(r)/ *n.* 正方形；二次幂

- **E** a shape with four straight sides of equal length and four angles of 90°; the number obtained when you multiply a number by itself
- **释** 正方形是有 4 条等长的直边和 4 个 90 度的角的形状；二次幂是一个数字与自身相乘时得到的数字。

016 **cube** /kjuːb/ *n.* 立方体；三次幂

- **E** a solid or hollow figure with six equal square sides; the number that you get when you multiply a number by itself twice
- **释** 立方体是一个由 6 个相等的正方形组成的实心或空心的图形；三次幂是一个数字乘以自身两次后得到的数字。

017 **rational** /ˈræʃnəl/ **number** 有理数

- **E** a number that can be expressed as the ratio of two whole numbers
- **释** 有理数是可以表示为两个整数之比的数。

018 **irrational** /ɪˈræʃnəl/ **number** 无理数

- **E** a number, for example π or the square root of 2, that cannot be expressed as the ratio of two whole numbers.
- **释** 无理数是不能表示为两个整数之比的数，例如 π 或 $\sqrt{2}$。

019 **series** /'sɪəriːz/ *n.* 级数

[E] the sum of the sequence

[释] 级数是数列的和。

020 **sequence** /'siːkwəns/ *n.* 数列

[E] a set whose elements have been listed in a particular order

[释] 数列是一组以特定的顺序排列的元素集合。

[易] series *n.* 级数

- e.g. 1, 2, 3, 4, 5... is the sequence; 1+2+3+4+5+... is the series.
- 例如，1，2，3，4，5……是数列；1+2+3+4+5+……则是级数。

021 **approximation** /əˌprɒksɪ'meɪʃn/ *n.* 近似值，近似法

[E] an estimate of a number or an amount that is almost correct, but not exact

[释] 近似值是一个估值或一个几乎正确但又不完全准确的数额。

022 **estimate** /'estɪmət/ *n.* 估计

/'estɪmeɪt/ *v.* 估计

[E] a judgement that you make without having the exact details or figures about the size, amount, cost, etc

[释] 估计是在没有关于尺寸、金额、成本等的确切信息或数字的情况下做出的判断。

023 **significant** /sɪg'nɪfɪkənt/ **figure** /'fɪgə(r)/ 有效数字

[E] each of the digits in a number that are needed in order to give it accurately; For example, 0.123 (3 significant figure) and 1.230 (4 significant figure).

[释] 数字中的每一个数位都是必需的，都是为了让数字更准确，例如，0.123（3 个有效数字）和 1.230（4 个有效数字）。

024 ratio /ˈreɪʃiəʊ/   *n.* 比率

- 📖 the relationship between two groups of people or things that is represented by two numbers showing how much larger one group is than the other
- 释 比率是指两组人或事物之间的关系,用两个数字来表示一组比另一组大多少。

025 proportion /prəˈpɔːʃn/   *n.* 比例,倍数关系

- 📖 the relationship of one thing to another in size, amount, etc
- 释 比例是指事物在大小、数量等方面与另一事物的关系。

026 percentage /pəˈsentɪdʒ/   *n.* 百分比

- 📖 the number, amount, rate of something, expressed as if it is part of a total which is 100; a part or share of a whole
- 释 百分比是指把某物的数目、数量、比率假设为总数 100 的一部分表示出来,指整体的一部分或一份。

027 interest /ˈɪntrəst/   *n.* 利息

- 📖 the extra money that you pay back when you borrow money or that you receive when you invest money
- 释 利息是你向别人借钱时需要额外偿还的钱,或你投资时赚到的本金以外的钱。
- 扩 simple interest 单利
  - Interest that is paid only on the original amount of money that you invested, and not on any interest that it has earned.
  - 单利是指不加入任何赚取的利息,只按投资的原始金额支付利息。

  compound interest 复利
  - Interest that is paid both on the original amount of money saved and on the interest that has been added to it.
  - 复利是指按储蓄的原始金额和已经赚取的利息来支付利息。

028 **constant** /'kɒnstənt/ *n.* 常数

[E] a number or quantity that does not vary; For example, 5 is a constant but 5*x* is a variable.

[释] 常数是不变的数或量。例如，5 是常数，而 5*x* 则是变量。

029 **calculator** /'kælkjuleɪtə(r)/ *n.* 计算器

[E] a small electronic device for calculating with numbers

[释] 计算器是一种可以进行数字计算的小型电子装置。

030 **reciprocal** /rɪ'sɪprəkl/ *n.* 倒数

[E] the fraction obtained when the values of the numerator and denominator are interchanged

[释] 倒数是分子和分母的数值互换后得到的分数。

031 **bracket** /'brækɪt/ *n.* 括号

[E] either of a pair of marks, (), placed around extra information in a piece of writing or part of a problem in mathematics

[释] 括号是指在文章或数学问题中，把额外信息括起来的一对标记。

032 **lowest common multiple** 最小公倍数

[E] the smallest number except 0 that a group of numbers can be divided into exactly; e.g. The lowest common multiple of 10 and 25 is 50.

[释] 最小公倍数是两个或多个整数公有的倍数中除 0 以外最小的数。例如，10 和 25 的最小公倍数是 50。

033 **highest common factor** 最大公因数

[E] the highest number that can be divided exactly into two or more numbers; e.g. The highest common factor of 10 and 25 is 5.

[释] 最大公因数是两个或多个整数同时均能整除的整数中最小的数。例如，10 和 25 的最大公因数是 5。

第二小节　Algebra and Graph 代数和图形

扫一扫
听本节音频

034　**simplify** /ˈsɪmplɪfaɪ/　　　　　　　　*vt.* 简化

- 🄔 the method to make the fraction easier to understand or read
- 🄡 简化是一种使分数更容易理解或阅读的方法。

035　**linear** /ˈlɪniə(r)/　　　　　　　　*adj.* 线性的

- 🄔 able to be represented by a straight line on a graph.
- 🄡 线性的指可以用图形上的直线来表示。
- 🄥 non-linear *adj.* 非线性的

036　**consecutive** /kənˈsekjətɪv/　　*adj.* 连续不断的，连贯的

- 🄔 following one after another in a series, without interruption
- 🄡 连续不断的即一个接一个，连续不断，没有中断。
- 🄧 consecutive integer 连续的整数
  - e.g. 5, 6, 7, 8, 9... are the consecutive integers.
  - 例如，5、6、7、8、9……是连续的整数。

037　**elimination** /ɪˌlɪmɪˈneɪʃn/　　　　*n.* 消元

- 🄔 the act of removing an unknown mathematical quantity by combining equations
- 🄡 消元是通过合并方程来消除一个未知的数学量的方法。

038　**simultaneous equation**　　　　联立方程组

- 🄔 a finite set of equations for which common solutions are sought, e.g.

$$\begin{cases} x+2y=5 \\ 3x-y=1 \end{cases} \text{ or } \begin{cases} x^2+y^2=5 \\ x-2y=1 \end{cases}$$

- 🄡 联立方程组是一组有限的方程组，需要找出共同的解，即：

$$\begin{cases} x+2y=5 \\ 3x-y=1 \end{cases} \text{ 或 } \begin{cases} x^2+y^2=5 \\ x-2y=1 \end{cases}$$

039 **substitute** /ˈsʌbstɪtjuːt/   *v.* 代替

- **E** to replace one value with another (usually a letter with a number)
- **释** 代替是用一个值替换另一个值（通常是一个带数字的字母）。
- **扩** substitution *n.* 代替
  - the replacement of one mathematical entity by another of equal value
  - 代替是用一个等值的数学实体替换另一个数学实体。

040 **factorise** /ˈfæktəraɪz/   *vt.* 因式分解

- **E** to express a number in terms of its factors
- **释** 因式分解是用一个数的因数来表示这个数。
- **扩** factorisation *n.* 因式分解
  - re-writing an expression using brackets; For example, $2x^2 - 3x + 1 = (2x-1)(x-1)$.
  - 因式分解是指用括号重写表达式。例如，$2x^2 - 3x + 1 = (2x-1)(x-1)$。

041 **quadratic** /kwɒˈdrætɪk/ **expression** /ɪkˈspreʃn/
二次表达式

- **E** an expression where one term has a variable squared (and no variable with a higher power); for example, $ax^2 + bx + c$
- **释** 在二次表达式中，其中一项为一个变量的平方（没有具有更高幂的变量）。例如，$ax^2 + bx + c$。

042 **quadratic** /kwɒˈdrætɪk/ **equation** /ɪˈkweɪʒn/
二次方程

- **E** an equation that contains a quadratic expression; for example, $ax^2 + bx + c = 0$
- **释** 二次方程是包含二次表达式的方程。例如，$ax^2 + bx + c = 0$。

043 **quadratic** /kwɒˈdrætɪk/ **formula** /ˈfɔːmjələ/
二次公式

- Ⓔ the formula $\dfrac{-b \pm \sqrt{b^2 - 4ac}}{2a}$, which is used to find the roots of quadratic equation
- 释 二次公式是公式 $\dfrac{-b \pm \sqrt{b^2 - 4ac}}{2a}$，用于求二次方程的根。

044 **completing** /kəmˈpliːtɪŋ/ **the square** /skweə(r)/
配方法，完全平方

- Ⓔ a method to solve the quadratic equation
- 释 配方法是解二次方程的一种方法。

045 **intersection** /ˌɪntəˈsekʃn/
n. 交叉，交叉点

- Ⓔ a point where two or more lines meet or cross each other
- 释 交叉点是两条或多条线相交或交叉的点。

046 **index** /ˈɪndeks/
n. 指数

- Ⓔ the small number written above a larger number to show how many times that number must be multiplied by itself; For example, in the equation $4^2=16$, the number 2 is an index.
- 释 指数是写在较大数字右上方的小数字，表示该数字与自身相乘多少次。例如，在方程 $4^2=16$ 中，2 是指数。

047 **operation** /ˌɒpəˈreɪʃn/
n. 计算

- Ⓔ a process in which a number or quantity is changed by adding, multiplying, etc
- 释 计算是通过加、乘等方法改变一个数、量的过程。

048 **variable** /ˈveəriəbl/
n. 变量

- Ⓔ able to be changed
- 释 变量是可以改变的数。

049 **directly** /dəˈrektli/ **proportional** /prəˈpɔːʃənl/
成正比

- **E** Given two variables x and y, the variable y is directly proportional to x if there is a non-zero constant k; The relation is often denoted using the symbols ' $\propto$ '.
- 释 给定两个变量 x 和 y,如果存在一个非零常数 k,使得 $y = kx$,则变量 y 与 x 成正比。这种关系通常用符号 " $\propto$ " 表示。

050 **inversely** /ˌɪnˈvɜːsli/ **proportional** /prəˈpɔːʃənl/
成反比

- **E** Given two variables x and y, the variable y is inversely proportional to the variable x if there exists a non-zero constant k such that $y = \dfrac{k}{x}$.
- 释 给定两个变量 x 和 y,如果存在一个非零常数 k,使得 $y = \dfrac{k}{x}$,则变量 y 与变量 x 成反比。

051 **nth** /enθ/ **root**
n 次方根

- **E** The nth root of a number x, where n is usually assumed to be a positive integer, is a number r, when raised to the power n yields, where n is the degree of the root.
- 释 一个数字 x 的 n 次方根(n 通常是一个正整数)是一个数字 r。数字 r 的 n 次幂是 x,即 $r^n = x$,其中 n 是根的次数。
- 扩 square root 平方根
  - a number which when multiplied by itself produces a particular number, e.g. The square root of 64 is 8.
  - 平方根是一个数字将其乘以自身得出一个特定的数字,例如,64 的平方根是 8。

052 **power** /ˈpaʊə(r)/
n. 幂

- **E** the number of times that an amount is to be multiplied by itself, e.g. 4 to the power of 3 is 64.
- 释 幂是一个量要与自身相乘的次数。例如,4 的 3 次幂等于 64。

053 **inequality** /ˌɪnɪˈkwɒləti/ *n.* 不等式

[E] a relation which makes a non-equal comparison between two numbers or other mathematical expressions

[释] 不等式是两个数字或其他数学表达式之间进行不相等比较的关系。

[扩] The notation $a < b$ means that *a* is less than *b*.

符号 $a < b$ 即 a 小于 b。

The notation $a > b$ means that *a* is greater than *b*.

符号 $a > b$ 即 a 大于 b。

The notation $a \leq b$ means that *a* is less than or equal to *b* (or not greater than *b*).

符号 $a \leq b$ 即 a 小于或等于 b（即不大于 b）。

The notation $a \geq b$ means that a is greater than or equal to *b* (or not less than *b*).

符号 $a \geq b$ 即 a 大于或等于 b（即不少于 b）。

054 **number line** 数值轴

[E] a picture of a graduated straight line that serves as abstraction for real numbers

[释] 数值轴是一条有刻度的直线，可以把实数抽象表示出来。

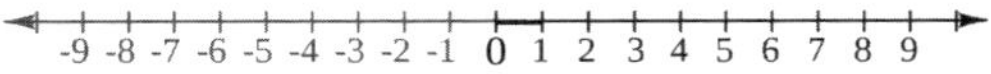
-9 -8 -7 -6 -5 -4 -3 -2 -1 0 1 2 3 4 5 6 7 8 9

055 **graphical** /ˈɡræfɪkl/ *adj.* 绘画的，用图表示的

[E] in the form of a diagram or graph

[释] 绘图的即以图表的形式来表示的。

056 **linear** /ˈlɪniə(r)/ **programming** /ˈprəʊɡræmɪŋ/ 线性规划

[E] a technique used in economics, etc, for determining the maximum or minimum of a linear function of non-negative variables subject to constraints expressed as linear equalities or inequalities

[释] 线性规划是一种用于经济学等领域的技术，用于确定受线性等式或不等式约束的非负变量的线性函数的最大值或最小值。

057 composite /'kɒmpəzɪt/ function /'fʌŋkʃn/ 复合函数

- **E** a function obtained from two given functions by applying first one function and then applying the second function to the result
- **释** 复合函数是通过应用第一个函数，然后对结果应用第二个函数，由这两个给定函数获得的函数。

058 inverse /ˌɪn'vɜːs/ function 反函数

- **E** a function obtained by expressing the dependent variable of one function as the independent variable of another; f and g are inverse functions if $f(x)=y$ and $g(y)=x$.
- **释** 反函数是把一个函数的因变量表示为另一个函数的自变量得到的函数。在 $f(x)=y$ 和 $g(y)=x$ 中，f 和 g 是反函数。

059 input value 输入值

- **E** the value input into a function; e.g. -2, -1, 0... can be input value in function $y=x^2$.
- **释** 输入值是输入到函数中的值。例如，x 为 -2, -1, 0……是函数 $y=x^2$ 的输入值。

060 output value 输出值

- **E** the value output from a function; e.g. 4, 1, 0... can be corresponding output value in the function $y=x^2$ when x is -2, -1, 0... respectively.
- **释** 输出值是从函数输出的值。例如，当 x 为 -2, -1, 0……时，4, 1, 0……分别是函数 $y=x^2$ 相应的输出值。

第三小节　Coordinate Geometry 坐标几何

061　**parallel** /ˈpærəlel/　　　*n.* 平行线
　　　　　　　　　　　　　　　　vt. 与……平行

- 英 two or more lines that are parallel to each other are the same distance apart at every point
- 释 平行线是指两条或多条相互平行的直线,一条直线上的任意一点到另一直线的距离相等。

062　**perpendicular** /ˌpɜːpənˈdɪkjələ(r)/　　*adj.* 垂直的
　　　　　　　　　　　　　　　　　　　　　　n. 垂直

- 英 forming an angle of 90° with another line or surface, vertical and going straight up
- 释 垂直的即与另一条直线或表面形成 90 度角,垂直并笔直向上。

063　**tangent** /ˈtændʒənt/　　*n.* 切线
　　　　　　　　　　　　　　　adj. 切线的

- 英 a straight line that touches the outside of a curve but does not cross it
- 释 切线是与曲线外表面相切但不穿过它的直线。

The straight line is the tangent line of the curve $y = x^2$.
直线是曲线 $y = x^2$ 的切线。→

064　**bisector** /baɪˈsektə/　　*n.* 平分线

- 英 a straight line or plane that bisects an angle or a line segment
- 释 平分线是平分角或线段的直线或平面。
- 扩 bisect *vt.* 平分,二等分
  - to divide something into two equal parts
  - 平分即把某物分成相等的两部分。

065 **perpendicular bisector** 垂直平分线，中垂线

[E] a line segment bisector, passing through the mid-point of the segment perpendicularly

[释] 垂直平分线是线段的平分线，垂直通过线段的中点。

The line CP is the perpendicular bisector of the segment AB.
直线 CP 是线段 AB 的垂直平分线。→

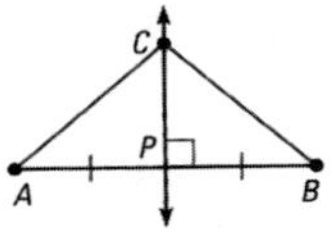

$CA = CB$

066 **gradient** /ˈgreɪdiənt/ *n.* 斜率

[E] the steepness of a line (or the steepness of a tangent drawn at a point on a curve)

[释] 斜率是直线的陡度（或曲线上一点的切线的陡度）。

[同] slope

067 **mid-point** /ˈmɪd pɔɪnt/ *n.* 中点

[E] exactly half way between the ends of a line segment

[释] 中点是在线段两端的正中间。

068 **coordinate** /kəʊˈɔːdɪnət/ *n.* 坐标

[E] either of two numbers or letters used to fix the position of a point on a map or graph

[释] 坐标是用来确定地图或图表上一个点的两上数字或字母。

[扩] *x*-coordinate *n.* *x* 轴坐标，横坐标

- a coordinate whose value is determined by measuring parallel to an *x*-axis
- *x* 轴坐标是与 *x* 轴平行的坐标，其值由测量值决定。

y-coordinate *n.* *y* 轴坐标，纵坐标

- a coordinate whose value is determined by measuring parallel to an *y*-axis.
- *y* 轴坐标是与 *y* 轴平行的坐标，其值由测量值决定。

Cartesian coordinate 笛卡尔坐标系

- a coordinate system that specifies each point uniquely in a plane by a set of numerical coordinates, which are the signed distances

to the point from two fixed perpendicular oriented lines, measured in the same unit of length
- 笛卡尔坐标系是一种通过一对数字坐标在平面中唯一地指定每个点的坐标系统，该坐标系是以相同的长度单位测量的两个固定的垂直有向线的点的有符号距离。

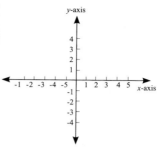

069 **axis** /ˈæksɪs/   *n.* 轴，坐标轴

- 🅔 A fixed line against which the positions of points are measured, especially points on a graph.
- 🅡 轴是测量点位置的固定线，尤指图上的点。
- 🅕 axes
- 🅧 *x*-axis *n.* *x* 轴，横坐标轴
  - the horizontal axis in a plane coordinate system
  - *x* 轴是平面坐标系中的水平轴。

  y-axis *n.* *y* 轴，纵坐标轴
  - the vertical axis in a plane coordinate system
  - *y* 轴是平面坐标系中的垂直轴。

070 **intersect** /ˌɪntəˈsekt/   *vi.* 相交

- 🅔 to meet or cross each other
- 🅡 相交是指互相交叉。
- 🅧 point of intersection 交点
  - a point where lines intersect
  - 交点是线相交的点。

071 **plot** /plɒt/   *vt.* 绘图，描点

- 🅔 to mark points on a graph and draw a line or curve connecting them
- 🅡 绘图是指在图上标记点，并画一条直线或曲线将这些点连起来。

072 **acceleration** /əkˌseləˈreɪʃn/   *n.* 加速度

- 🇬 the rate at which the velocity (= speed in a particular direction) of an object change
- 🇨 加速度是物体的速度（在特定方向上的速度）变化的速率。

073 **asymptote** /ˈæsɪm(p)təʊt/   *n.* 渐近线

- 🇬 a line that a graph approaches but never intersects; e.g. The asymptotes of the curve $y = \dfrac{1}{x}$ are x-axis and y-axis.
- 🇨 渐近线是图形接近但不相交的直线。例如，曲线 $y = \dfrac{1}{x}$ 的渐近线是 x 轴和 y 轴。

074 **exponential** /ˌekspəˈnenʃl/   *n.* 指数函数   *adj.* 指数的

- 🇬 A function formed when the variable is in the index. For example, a^x where a is a constant.
- 🇨 指数函数是变量为指数时形成的函数。例如，a^x 是指数函数，其中 a 为常数。

🔖 **exponential growth** 指数增长

- Exponential growth occurs when the growth rate of the value of a mathematical function is proportional to the function's current value.
- 数学函数值的增长率与函数当前值成正比时，指数增长会随之发生。

exponential decay 指数衰减

- Exponential decay occurs in the same way when the growth rate is negative.
- 当增长率为负值时，指数衰减会随之发生。

第四小节　Geometry 几何

075　**angle** /ˈæŋgl/　　　　　　　　　*n.* 角，角度

- **E** a measure of the amount of turning between two lines that meet at a point
- **释** 在某一点相交的两条线之间的回转量的量度。
- **扩** acute angle 锐角
  - an angle of less than 90°
  - 锐角是角度小于 90 度的角。

  obtuse angle 钝角
  - an angle between 90° and 180°
  - 钝角是角度在 90 度和 180 度之间的角。

  right angle 直角
  - an angle that is exactly 90°
  - 直角是角度为 90 度的角。

076　**triangle** /ˈtraɪæŋgl/　　　　　　*n.* 三角形

- **E** a flat shape with three straight sides and three angles
- **释** 具有三个角和三条边的平面图形。
- **扩** right-angled triangle 直角三角形
  - a triangle in which one angle is a right angle
  - 直角三角形是其中一个角是直角的三角形。

  isosceles triangle 等腰三角形
  - a triangle with two of its three sides the same length
  - 等腰三角形是三条边中的两条长度相等的三角形。

  equilateral triangle 等边三角形
  - a triangle whose three sides are all the same length
  - 等边三角形是三条边等长的三角形。

077　**quadrilateral** /ˌkwɒdrɪˈlætərəl/　*n.* 四边形

- **E** a flat shape with four straight sides
- **释** 四边形是同一平面上的四条直线所围成的图形。
- **扩** rectangle *n.* 长方形
  - a flat shape with four straight sides, two of which are longer than the other two, and four angles of 90°

- 长方形是由四条直线围成，其中两条比另两条长且四个角为90°的平面图形。

parallelogram *n.* 平行四边形
- a flat shape with four straight sides, the opposite sides being parallel and equal to each other
- 平行四边形是两对边平行且相等的四条直线所围成的平面图形。

trapezium *n.* 梯形
- a flat shape with four straight sides, one pair of opposite sides being parallel and the other pair not parallel
- 梯形是一组对边平行、另一组不平行的四条直边所围成的平面图形。

rhombus *n.* 菱形
- a flat shape with four equal sides and four angles which are not 90°, also diagonals are bisected and perpendicular
- 菱形是四条边等长和四个角不是直角的平面图形，其对角线互相垂直平分且平分每一组对角。

078 polygon /ˈpɒlɪɡən/   *n.* 多边形

英 a flat shape with at least three straight sides and angles, and usually five or more

汉 多边形是至少由三条直线和三个角围成的平面图形，通常为五条直线和五个角或者更多。

扩 pentagon *n.* 五边形
- a flat shape with five straight sides and five angles
- 五边形是具有五个角和五条边的平面图形。

hexagon *n.* 六边形
- a flat shape with six straight sides and six angles
- 六边形是有六条边和六个角的平面图形。

octagon *n.* 八边形
- a flat shape with eight straight sides and eight angles
- 八边形是有八条边和八个角的平面图形。

decagon *n.* 十边形
- a flat shape with ten straight sides and ten angles
- 十边形是有十条边和十个角的平面图形。

079 Pythagoras' /paɪˈθæɡərəsɪz/ theorem /ˈθɪərəm/

毕达哥拉斯定理，勾股定理

- **E** It states that the square of the hypotenuse (the side opposite the right angle) is equal to the sum of the squares of the other two sides, i.e. $a^2 + b^2 = c^2$.
- **释** 毕达哥拉斯定理是指斜边的平方（与直角相对的那一边）等于另外两边的平方之和，即 $a^2 + b^2 = c^2$。
- **扩** hypotenuse *n.* 直角三角形的斜边
  - the side opposite the right angle of a right-angled triangle
  - 直角三角形的斜边是与直角三角形直角相对的边。

080 symmetry /ˈsɪmətri/   *n.* 对称

- **E** having the same shape in different positions either through reflection in a line or rotation about a point
- **释** 对称是指沿一条直线对折或绕一点旋转后，位置改变但形状不变。
- **扩** symmetrical *adj.* 对称的
  - a shape that has a property of symmetry
  - 对称的即图形具有对称性的。

081 line symmetry   对称轴

- **E** a line that divides a plane shape into two halves so that one half is the mirror image of the other
- **释** 对称轴是把一个平面形状分成两半使其中一半是另一半的镜像的线。
- **同** axis of symmetry

082 rotation /rəʊˈteɪʃn/   *n.* 旋转

- **E** a transformation that creates an image by rotating points by a given angle about a fixed point
- **释** 旋转是通过把一些点按照特定角度围绕定点旋转来产生图像的一种变换。

- **rotational symmetry** 旋转对称
  - turning a shape about a fixed point so that it looks the same in different positions
  - 旋转对称是指把图形围绕一个定点旋转，使其在不同位置看起来相同。

083 **plane** /pleɪn/   *n.* 平面

- any flat or level surface, or an imaginary flat surface through or joining material objects
- 平面是指任何平面、水平面和通过或连接实物的假想平面。
- **plane symmetry** 对称面
  - a flat surface that cuts a solid into two halves so that one half is the mirror image of the other
  - 对称面是把实心体切成两部分使一半是另一半镜像的平面。

084 **similarity** /ˌsɪməˈlærəti/   *n.* 类似，相似

- the state of being like something but not exactly the same
- 类似是指与某物相像但不完全相同的状态。

085 **congruence** /ˈkɒŋɡruəns/   *n.* 全等

- figures that are identical in both shape and size
- 全等是指形状和大小都相同的图形。

086 **scale** /skeɪl/   *n.* 比例

- proportion
- a ratio that indicates how much smaller (or larger) a drawing is from the original object
- 比例是表示图像比原来的物体小（或大）多少的比率。
- **scale factor of areas** 面积之比
  - the multiplying factor for the area of a shape that is enlarged from an original (the square of the multiplying factor for sides)
  - 面积之比是原始图形放大后的图形面积的倍数（即边长的乘数的平方）。

  scale factor of lengths 长度之比
  - the multiplying factor for the sides of a shape that is enlarged from an original
  - 长度之比是原始图形放大后的图形边长的倍数。

scale factor of volumes 体积之比
- the multiplying factor for the volume of a shape that is enlarged from an original (the cube of the multiplying factor for sides)
- 体积之比是原来的图形放大后的体积的倍数（即边长的乘数的立方）。

087 **dimension** /daɪˈmenʃn, dɪˈmenʃn/   *n.* 维

- **E** a measurement in space, for example the height, width or length of something
- **译** 维是在空间中的度量，例如某物的高度、宽度或长度。
- 扩 two dimensional 二维的
  - involving two dimensions
  - 二维的即涉及两个维度。

  three dimensional 三维的
  - involving three dimensions
  - 三维的即涉及三个维度。

088 **centre** /ˈsentə(r)/   *n.* 中心

- **E** the middle point or part of something, e.g. the centre of a circle
- **译** 中心是某物的中点或中间部分，例如，圆心。

第五小节 Measuration 测量

089 **circle** /ˈsɜːkl/   *n.* 圆

- **E** a set of (joined) points that are the same distance (radius) from a given fixed point (the centre)
- **译** 圆是到给定的定点（圆心）距离相同（半径）的一组（连接）点。
- 扩 semi-circle *n.* 半圆
  - one half of a circle, or something having the shape of half a circle
  - 半圆是圆的一半，或具有半圆形状的东西。

090 **perimeter** /pəˈrɪmɪtə(r)/   *n.* 周长

- **E** the distance around the edges of a plane shape
- **译** 周长是围绕平面图形一周的距离。
- 易 circumference *n.* 圆周

- the distance of a line that goes around a circle or any other curved shape
- 圆周是围绕一个圆或任何其他曲线图形运动一周的距离。

091 **diameter** /daɪˈæmɪtə(r)/   *n.* 直径

E a straight line going from one side of a circle or any other round object to the other side, passing through the centre

释 直径是从圆或任何圆形物体的一边穿过中心到另一边的一条直线。

扩 radius *n.* 半径
- a straight line between the centre of a circle and any point on its outer edge
- 半径是在圆的中心到圆的外缘上的任何点之间的一条直线。

092 **shaded** /ˈʃeɪdɪd/ **area**   阴影面积

E the area of a part of a drawing, etc, darker

释 阴影面积是如涂画的部分等较暗的区域。

093 **diagonal** /daɪˈæɡənl/   *n.* 对角线
adj. 斜的，对角线的

E a straight line connecting any two vertices of a polygon that are not adjacent

释 对角线是连接不相邻多边形任意两个顶点的直线。

094 **regular** /ˈreɡjələ(r)/ **polygon**   正多边形

E a polygon with each side of equal length

释 正多边形是五边等长的多边形。

扩 regular hexagon 正六边形
- a hexagon with six sides of equal length
- 正六边形是六边等长的六边形。

regular octagon 正八边形
- a octagon with eight sides of equal length
- 正八边形是八边等长的八边形。

095 **arc** /ɑːk/

n. 弧，弧形物
adj. 圆弧的

- 🇪 part of a circle or a curved line
- 🇨 弧是圆或曲线的一部分。
- 🔍 arc length 弧长
  - determining the length of an irregular arc segment, also called rectification of a curve
  - 弧长是确定不规则弧线的长度，也称为曲线整流。

096 **sector** /ˈsektə(r)/

n. 扇形

- 🇪 part of a circle defined by the angle that two radii make at the centre of the circle
- 🇨 扇形是由两个半径在圆心的夹角确定的圆的一部分。
- 🔍 sector area 扇形面积
  - the area of the part of a circle
  - 扇形面积是圆的一部分的面积。

097 **chord** /kɔːd/

n. 弦

- 🇪 a straight line that joins two points on a curve
- 🇨 弦是连接曲线上两点的直线。

098 **segment** /ˈsegmənt/

n. 部分

- 🇪 a part of something that is separate from the other parts or can be considered separately
- 🇨 部分是与其他部分分开或可以分开考虑的某物的一部分。

chord 是直线，segment 是阴影部分这块区域。→

099 **minor segment**

小弓形

- 🇪 the smaller of two circle segments formed when a chord is drawn between two points on the circumference
- 🇨 小弓形是圆周上两点间画弦时形成的两个弓形中较小的一个。

100 **major segment** 大弓形

- 🇬🇧 the larger of two circle segments formed when a chord is drawn between two points on the circumference
- 🇨🇳 大弓形是圆周上两点间画弦时形成的两个弓形中较大的一个。

101 **cross-section** /ˈkrɒsˌsekʃən/ *n.* 横截面

- 🇬🇧 A cross-section of an object is what you would see if you could cut straight through the middle of it.
- 🇨🇳 从一个物体的中间竖直切开就是横截面。

102 **prism** /ˈprɪzəm/ *n.* 棱柱

- 🇬🇧 a solid figure with ends that are parallel and of the same size and shape, and with sides whose opposite edges are equal and parallel
- 🇨🇳 棱柱是一种上下底面平行且大小和形状相同、侧棱平行且相等的立体图形。
- 扩 triangular prism 三棱柱
  - a prism whose base is triangle
  - 三棱柱是底边为三角形的棱柱。

103 **cuboid** /ˈkjuːbɔɪd/ *n.* 长方体

- 🇬🇧 a solid object which has six rectangular sides at right angles to each other
- 🇨🇳 长方体是有六个相互垂直的长方形侧面的立体图形。

104 **cylinder** /ˈsɪlɪndə(r)/ *n.* 圆柱

- 🇬🇧 a solid or hollow figure with round ends and long straight sides
- 🇨🇳 圆柱是两端是圆形和长方形侧面围成的实心或空心立体图形。

105 **pyramid** /ˈpɪrəmɪd/ *n.* 棱锥体；金字塔

[E] a solid shape with a square or triangular base and sloping sides that meet in a point at the top

[释] 棱锥体是由一个正方形底面和四个相交于顶点的三角形斜面的立体图形。

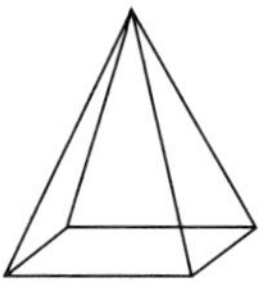

106 **cone** /kəʊn/ *n.* 圆锥体

[E] a solid or hollow object with a round flat base and sides that slope up to a point

[释] 圆锥体是由平面的圆形底面和由底面边缘倾斜到一点形成的侧面构成的实心或空心的立体图形。

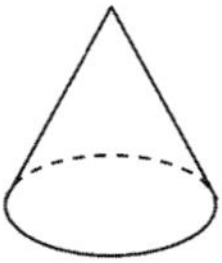

107 **sphere** /sfɪə(r)/ *n.* 球体

[E] a solid figure that is completely round, with every point on its surface at an equal distance from the centre

[释] 球体是表面上的每一点与中心的距离相等的圆形的实心图形。

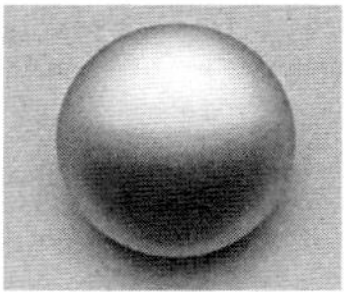

108 **surface area** 表面积

[E] The surface area of a solid object is a measure of the total area that the surface of an object occupies.

[释] 表面积是立体物总面积的尺度，即物体表面所占的面积。

109 **slant** /slɑːnt/ **height** 斜高

[E] the length of an element of a right circular cone

[释] 斜高是正圆锥体中一条母线的长度。

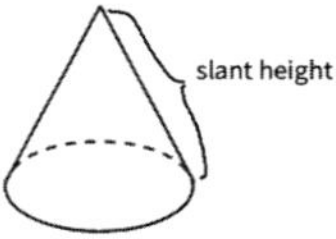

第六小节　Trigonometry 三角函数

扫一扫
听本节音频

110　**hypotenuse** /haɪˈpɒtənjuːz/　　*n.* 直角三角形的斜边

- 🇪 the longest side of a right-angled triangle
- 释 直角三角形的斜边是直角三角形的最长边。

111　**opposite** /ˈɒpəzɪt/　　*n.* 对边

- 🇪 a 'shorter' side of a right-angled triangle that is 'opposite' an angle other than the right-angle
- 释 在直角三角形中，除直角外的另外两个角所对的边称为这个角的对边，比斜边短。

112　**adjacent** /əˈdʒeɪsnt/　　*n.* 邻边

- 🇪 a 'shorter' side of a right-angled triangle that is next to an angle other than the right-angle
- 释 在直角三角形中，除直角外的另外两个角所相邻的边称为这个角的邻边，与斜边相比较短。

hypotenuse 是直角三角形的斜边，opposite 是 θ 的对边，adjacent 是 θ 的邻边

113　**enlargement** /ɪnˈlɑːdʒmənt/　　*n.* 放大

- 🇪 something that has been made larger
- 释 放大是指某物变大。

114　**trigonometry** /ˌtrɪɡəˈnɒmətri/　　*n.* 三角学

- 🇪 the study of the properties of triangles and trigonometric functions and of their applications
- 释 三角学是三角形和三角函数的性质及其应用的研究。

- 扩 trigonometric function 三角函数
  - any of a group of functions of an angle expressed as a ratio of two of the sides of a right-angled triangle containing the angle
  - 三角函数是一个角以所在的直角三角形的两条边之比的形式表示出来的一组函数。

115 **sine** /saɪn/   *n.* 正弦

- 英 the ratio of the length of the side opposite one of the angles in a right-angled triangle that are less than 90° to the length of the longest side
- 释 正弦是在直角三角形中，一个锐角对边的长度与最长边的长度之比。

$$\sin\theta = \frac{\text{opposite}}{\text{hypotenuse}}$$

116 **cosine** /ˈkəʊsaɪn/   *n.* 余弦

- 英 the ratio of the length of the side next to an acute angle in a right-angled triangle to the length of the longest side
- 释 余弦是在直角三角形中，与锐角相邻的边的长度与最长边的长度之比。

$$\cos\theta = \frac{\text{adjacent}}{\text{hypotenuse}}$$

117 **tangent** /ˈtændʒənt/   *n.* 正切

- 英 the ratio of the length of the side opposite an angle in a right-angled triangle to the length of the side next to it
- 释 正切是在直角三角形中，一个角的对边长度与相邻边的长度之比。

$$\tan\theta = \frac{\text{opposite}}{\text{adjacent}}$$

118 **clockwise** /ˈklɒkwaɪz/   *adj.* 顺时针方向的

- 英 moving around in the same direction as the hands of a clock
- 释 顺时针方向的即与钟表的指针移动的方向一致。
- 易 anticlockwise *adj.* 逆时针方向的
  - in the opposite direction to the movement of the hands of a clock
  - 逆时针方向的即和钟表的指针移动的方向相反。

119 **bearing** /ˈbeərɪŋ/ — *n.* 方位角

- **E** an angle indicating the direction of travel between two points; The bearing begins from the 'North' direction and is measured clockwise round to the line joining start point and destination.
- **释** 方位角即表示两点之间运动方向的角。方位角是从直线起点的标准方向北端起,顺时针方向量到直线的角度。

120 **sine rule** — 正弦定理

- **E** In trigonometry, sine rule is an equation relating the lengths of the sides of any shaped triangle to the sines of its angles.
- **释** 在三角学中,正弦定理把任意形状的三角形边长与其内角正弦值联系起来。

121 **cosine rule** — 余弦定理

- **E** In trigonometry, cosine rule relates the lengths of the sides of a triangle to the cosine of one of its angles.
- **释** 在三角学中,余弦定理把三角形边长与其中一个角的余弦值联系起来。

122 **equidistant** /ˌiːkwɪˈdɪstənt/ — *adj.* 等距的

- **E** A point is said to be equidistant from a set of objects if the distances between that point and each object in the set are equal.
- **释** 等距的即如果一个点到一组中每个物体的距离相等,则称该点到该组物体的距离相等。

第七小节 Vectors and Transformation 向量和变形

扫一扫
听本节音频

123 **matrix** /ˈmeɪtrɪks/ *n.* 矩阵

[E] an arrangement of numbers, symbols, etc, in rows and columns, treated as a single quantity

[释] 矩阵是一种把数字、符号等排列成行、列作为一个单独的量来处理的方法。

[复] matrices

[扩] matrix operation 矩阵运算

- a mathematical operation involving matrices
- 矩阵运算是涉及矩阵的数学运算。

124 **vector** /ˈvektə(r)/ *n.* 向量；矢量

[E] a quantity that has both size and direction

[释] 向量即有大小和方向的量。

[易] scalar *n.* 标量

- a quantity having size but no direction
- 标量即有大小但没有方向的量。

125 **column** /ˈkɒləm/ **vector** 列向量

[E] In linear algebra, a column vector or column matrix is an $m \times 1$ matrix, i.e. a matrix consisting of a single column of m elements.

[释] 在线性代数中，列向量或列矩阵是 $m \times 1$ 矩阵，即由 m 个元素组成的单列矩阵。

126 **position** /pəˈzɪʃn/ **vector** 位置向量

[E] In geometry, a position vector is a Euclidean vector that represents the position of a point P in space in relation to an arbitrary reference origin O.

[释] 在几何中，位置向量是一个欧氏向量，表示空间中点 P 相对于任意参考原点 O 的位置。

127　**base vector**　　　　　　　　　　　　基向量

- **英** Base vectors are $\begin{pmatrix}1\\0\end{pmatrix}$ and $\begin{pmatrix}0\\1\end{pmatrix}$.
- **释** 基向量是 $\begin{pmatrix}1\\0\end{pmatrix}$ 和 $\begin{pmatrix}0\\1\end{pmatrix}$。

128　**modulus** /ˈmɒdjʊləs/　　　　　　*n.* 模数；绝对值

- **英** the magnitude of the number without a sign attached; The modulus of a number is also called the absolute value.
- **释** 模数即去掉正负号的数字的大小。一个数的模也叫绝对值。

129　**flow diagram** /ˈdaɪəɡræm/　　　　　　流程图

- **英** a diagram of the sequence of operations in a computer program or an accounting system
- **释** 流程图是计算机程序或会计系统中显示操作顺序的图表。

130　**determinant** /dɪˈtɜːmɪnənt/　　　　　*n.* 行列式

- **英** In a two by two matrix, the product of the elements in the leading diagonal minus the product of the elements in the other diagonal.
- **释** 行列式是在一个 2×2 矩阵中，主对角线上元素的乘积减去另一个对角线上元素的乘积。

131　**transformation** /ˌtrænsfəˈmeɪʃn/　　*n.* 变换，变形

- **英** a function that changes the position or direction of the axes of a coordinate system
- **释** 变换是指改变坐标系中坐标轴的位置或方向的函数。
- **扩** combined transformation 组合变换
  - one transformation followed by another transformation
  - 组合变换即一个变换之后还有另一个变换。

132 reflection /rɪ'flekʃn/ *n.* 反射

[E] a transformation that creates an image by reflecting points a given line

[释] 反射即通过在给定的直线上反射点来产生图像的一种变换。

133 translation /trænz'leɪʃn/ *n.* 平移

[E] a transformation that creates an image of a point by 'sliding' it along a plane

[释] 平移是一种通过沿平面"滑动"来创建点的图像的变换。

134 shear /ʃɪə(r)/ *n.* 切变

[E] a deformation of an object in which parallel planes remain parallel but are shifted in a direction parallel to themselves (The area is the same.)

[释] 切变是物体的形变，其平行的平面保持平行，但向与之平行的方向上移动（面积不变）。

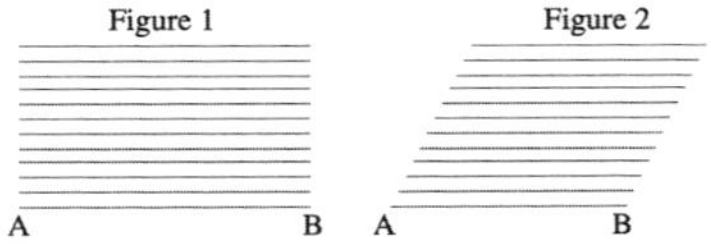

The area is thesame after a shear.
面积在切变后保持不变。

135 stretch /stretʃ/ *v.* 拉长

[E] to make something longer or wider (The area may be changed.)

[释] 拉长是使某物变长或变宽（面积可能会改变）。

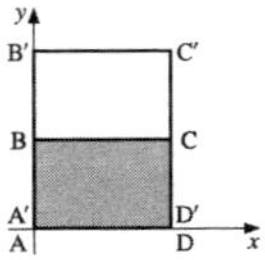

Stretch factor 2 parallel to the y-axis, invariant line $y = 0$.
伸缩因子 2 平行于 y 轴，即不变直线 $y = 0$。

136 **colinear** /kəʊˈlɪnɪə/   *adj.* 共线的

- **E** a set of points lying on a single line
- **释** 共线的即一组点的共线，在同一条线上。

137 **coplanar** /kəʊˈpleɪnə/   *adj.* 共面的

- **E** In geometry, a set of points in space are coplanar if there exists a geometric plane that contains them all.
- **释** 在几何中，如果一组点同在一个几何平面，那么空间中的这组点就是共面的。

第二节
Statistics 统计

扫一扫
听本节音频

第一小节　Probability 概率

138　**probability** /ˌprɒbəˈbɪləti/　　*n.* 概率，可能性

- **E** how likely something to happen
- **释** 概率即事情发生可能性的大小。
- **同** likelihood

139　**set** /set/　　*n.* 集合

- **E** a list or collection of objects that share a characteristic
- **释** 集合即具有相同特征的对象的列表或集合。

140　**element** /ˈelɪmənt/　　*n.* 元素

- **E** a member of a set
- **释** 元素即集合中的一员。

141　**subset** /ˈsʌbset/　　*n.* 子集

- **E** a set whose elements are all also members of another (usually larger) set
- **释** 子集作为一个集合，其元素也是另一个（较大）集合的成员。

142　**intersection** /ˈɪntəsekʃn/　　*n.* 交集

- **E** the set of elements common to two or more sets; A intersect B written as $A \cap B$
- **释** 交集是两个或多个集合共有的元素集合。集合 A 与集合 B 的交集写作 $A \cap B$。

143 **union** /ˈjuːniən/   *n.* 并集

- 🄴 a set containing all and only the members of two or more given sets; A union B written as $A \cup B$.
- 🄷 并集是包含两个或多个给定集合的所有成员的集合。集合 A 与集合 B 的并集写作 $A \cup B$。

144 **universal** /ˌjuːnɪˈvɜːsl/ **set**   泛集

- 🄴 for a given problem, all the elements that could possibly be included
- 🄷 泛集是可能包含既定问题相关的所有元素的集合。

145 **empty set**   空集

- 🄴 a set that contains no elements; Usually written as Ø.
- 🄷 空集是不包含元素的集合，通常写为 Ø。

146 **complement** /ˈkɒmplɪment/   *n.* 补集

- 🄴 the elements that are in the universal set but not in a given set
- 🄷 补集是在通用集合中但不在给定集合中的元素。

147 **Venn diagram** /ˈdaɪəɡræm/   维恩图

- 🄴 a pictorial method for illustrating the elements and interconnections of sets
- 🄷 维恩图是一种用于说明集合的元素和相互联系的图示方法。

148 **region** /ˈriːdʒən/   *n.* 区间

- 🄴 a region in a plane that satisfies a set linear inequality
- 🄷 区间是平面上满足一组线性不等式的集合区间。

149 **outcome** /ˈaʊtkʌm/   *n.* 结果

- 🄴 a possible results of an 'experiment'
- 🄷 结果是"实验"可能得出的结果。

150 **trial** /'traɪəl/ *n.* 试验

[E] an 'experiment' to determine the value of an outcome

[释] 试验是一种确定结果价值的"实验"。

151 **dice** /'daɪs/ *n.* 骰子

[E] a small cube of wood, plastic, etc., with a different number of spots on each of its sides, used in games of chance

[释] 骰子是一种用木头、塑料等制成的小立方体，每一面有不同数量的圆点，用于博运气。

[同] die

152 **fair** /feə(r)/ *adj.* 公平的

[E] not favouring any particular outcome, object or person

[释] 公平的指不偏向任何特定结果、对象或人。

[反] unfair *adj.* 不公平的

153 **bias** /'baɪəs/ *n.* 偏差

[E] The design of a statistical study shows bias if it would consistently underestimate or consistently overestimate the value you want to know.

[释] 如果一项统计研究的设计总是低估或高估你想知道的价值，就会出现偏差。

154 **mutually** /'mjuːtʃuəli/ **exclusive** /ɪk'skluːsɪv/ 互斥的

[E] not happening at the same time

[释] 互斥的即不可能同时发生的。

155 **independent** /ˌɪndɪ'pendənt/ **event** 独立事件

[E] an event whose outcome is not affected/influenced by what has occurred before

[释] 独立事件即结果不受以前发生的事情影响的事件。

156 **tree diagram** 树状图

- ☒ representing the outcomes from a multi-step experiment
- ㊗ 树状图用以表示多步骤实验的结果。

157 **conditional** /kənˈdɪʃənl/ **probability** 条件概率

- ☒ the probability that a given event will occur if it is certain that another event has taken place or will take place
- ㊗ 如果确定已经发生或将要发生另一事件,则某一事件发生的概率是条件概率。

第二小节 Data Representation 数据表示法

扫一扫
听本节音频

158 **pie chart** 饼状图

- ☒ a circular chart which uses slices or sectors of the circle to show the data
- ㊗ 饼状图即使用圆形的切片或扇区来显示数据的一种圆形图表。

159 **discrete** /dɪˈskriːt/ **data** 离散数据

- ☒ data that can only take certain (usually integer) values, for example: the number of people, the number of pens, etc.
- ㊗ 离散数据是只能获取某些值(通常是整数)的数据,例如,人数、笔的数量等。

160 **continuous** /kənˈtɪnjuəs/ **data** 连续数据

- ☒ data that can take any value in a range, such as height or weight, etc
- ㊗ 连续数据是可以取范围内任何值的数据,例如身高或体重等。

161 **bar chart** 柱状图

- ☒ a diagram used to display discrete data
- ㊗ 柱状图即用来显示离散数据的图表。

162 **spreadsheet** /ˈspredʃiːt/   *n.* 电子数据表

E a computer program that is used, for example, when doing financial or project planning
释 电子数据表是在做财务或项目计划等情况下使用的一种计算机程序。

163 **scatter** /ˈskætə(r)/ **graph**   点状图

E a scatter graph is a type of mathematical diagram using Cartesian coordinates to display values for two variables for a set of data
释 点状图是一种使用笛卡尔坐标来显示一组数据的两个变量值的数学图表。

164 **histogram** /ˈhɪstəgræm/   *n.* 直方图

E a specialised graph used to illustrate grouped continuous data
释 直方图即专门用于说明分组的连续数据的图表。

165 **frequency** /ˈfriːkwənsi/ **table**   频率表

E a method of summarising data when values or classes occur more than once
释 频率表是当值或类不止一次出现时,对数据进行汇总的一种方法。

166 **frequency density** /ˈdensəti/   频率密度

E the frequency of a class divided by the width of the class
释 频率密度即类的频率除以组宽。

167 **mean** /miːn/   *n.* 平均数

E an average that uses all the data
释 平均数即所有数据的平均值。

168 **median** /ˈmiːdiən/   *n.* 中位数

- 🇪 an average, the middle value of data when it is arranged in increasing order
- 🇨 中位数即数据按递增顺序排列时的中间值。

169 **mode** /məʊd/   *n.* 众数

- 🇪 an average, the most frequently occurring value in a set of data
- 🇨 众数是一组数据中出现频率最高的数值。
- 🇫 modal class 众数组
  - For grouped data, a class that has the highest frequency.
  - 众数组是分组数据中具有最高频率的那一组。

170 **bivariate** /baɪˈveərɪət/   *adj.* 双变量的

- 🇪 involving two random variables, not necessarily independent of one another
- 🇨 双变量的即包含两个随机变量但不一定相互独立的量。

171 **correlation** /ˌkɒrəˈleɪʃn/   *n.* 相关，关联

- 🇪 the relationship between bivariate data
- 🇨 相关即双变量之间的关系。

172 **cumulative** /ˈkjuːmjələtɪv/ **frequency** 累积频数

- 🇪 a 'running total' of the frequencies
- 🇨 累积频数即频数的累加总数。

173 **percentile** /pəˈsentaɪl/   *n.* 百分位

- 🇪 the value of data at a specified position (the data must be arranged in increasing order)
- 🇨 百分位是指定位置数据的值（数据必须按递增顺序排列）。

174 **lower quartile** /ˈkwɔːtaɪl/   下四分位数，Q_1

- 🇪 the value of data at the 25th percentile
- 🇨 下四分位数即数据在 25% 时的值。

175 upper quartile — 上四分位数，$Q3$

- 🇪 the value of data at the 75th percentile
- 🇨 上四分位数即数据在 75% 时的值。

176 interquartile /ˌɪntəˈkwɔːtaɪl/ range — 四分位距

- 🇪 the difference between the upper and lower quartiles, i.e. $Q_3 - Q_1$
- 🇨 四分位距是上四分位数和下四分位数之间的差，即 $Q_3 - Q_1$。

177 stem-and-leaf diagram — 茎叶图

- 🇪 a type of table for displaying ordered discrete data in rows with intervals of equal widths
- 🇨 茎叶图是用于以等宽的间隔显示行中的有序离散数据的一种表格。

```
5 | 3 5 8 8      Key: 5 | 3
6 | 1 1 2 4 7 9  represents
7 | 2 7 9        a score of 53
8 |
9 | 2 7
```

178 box-and-whisker /ˈwɪskə(r)/ plot /plɒt/ — 箱线图

- 🇪 a convenient way of graphically depicting groups of numerical data through their quartiles
- 🇨 箱线图是一种通过四分位数以图形方式描述数字数据组的便捷方法。

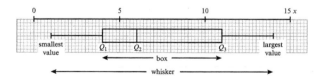

11~12 年级高频专业词汇

第一节

Pure Mathematics 纯数

扫一扫
听本节音频

第一小节 Algebra 代数

179 **parabola** /pə'ræbələ/ *n.* 抛物线

[E] the graph of a quadratic function

[释] 抛物线是二次函数的图像。

180 **stationary** /'steɪʃənri/ **point** 驻点

[E] a point on a curve where the gradient is zero

[释] 驻点是曲线上斜率为零的点。

[同] turning point

181 **vertex** /'vɜːteks/ *n.* 顶点

[E] the vertex of a parabola is the maximum or minimum point

[释] 抛物线的顶点是最大值或最小值点。

182 **discriminant** /dɪ'skrɪmɪnənt/ *n.* 判别式

[E] the part of the quadratic formula underneath the square root sign

[释] 判别式是在二次公式根号底下的部分。

183 **polynomial** /ˌpɒlɪˈnəʊmiəl/ — *n.* 多项式

- 🄔 an expression of the form $a_n x^n + a_{n-1} x^{n-1} + a_{n-2} x^{n-2} + ... + a_1 x^1 + a_0$
- 🄹 多项式是形式为 $a_n x^n + a_{n-1} x^{n-1} + a_{n-2} x^{n-2} + \cdots\cdots + a_1 x^1 + a_0$ 的表达式。

184 **degree** /dɪˈɡriː/ — *n.* 次

- 🄔 The highest power of x in the polynomial is called the degree of the polynomial. e.g. $3x^3 - 2x^2 + 1$ is a polynomial of degree 3.
- 🄹 多项式中 x 的最高次幂称为多项式的次。例如，$3x^3 - 2x^2 + 1$ 是次数为 3 的多项式。

185 **factor** /ˈfæktə(r)/ — *n.* 因数

- 🄔 a portion of a quantity that, when multiplied by other factors, gives the entire quantity
- 🄹 因数作为数的一部分，当与其他因数相乘时，得到全部的量。

186 **remainder** /rɪˈmeɪndə(r)/ — *n.* 余数

- 🄔 the amount left over after a division
- 🄹 余数是进行除法运算后剩余的数。

187 **dividend** /ˈdɪvɪdend/ — *n.* 被除数

- 🄔 the quantity being divided by another quantity.
- 🄹 被除数是除法运算中被另一个数所除的数。
- 🄺 divisor *n.* 除数
  - the quantity by which another quantity is to be divided
  - 除数是除法算式中除号后面的数。

188 **quotient** /ˈkwəʊʃnt/ — *n.* 商

- 🄔 a result obtained by dividing one quantity by another
- 🄹 商即除法运算得到的结果。
- 🄿 Division algorithm for polynomials:
  dividend = divisor × quotient + remainder
  多项式的除法：
  被除数 = 除数 × 商 + 余数

189 factor theorem /ˈθɪərəm/   因式定理

- 英 If for a polynomial $P(x)$, $P(c)=0$ then $x-c$ is a factor of $P(x)$.
- 释 因式定理即如果在一个多项式 $P(x)$ 中，$P(c)=0$，那么 $x-c$ 就是 $P(x)$ 的一个因数。

190 remainder /rɪˈmeɪndə(r)/ theorem   余式定理

- 英 If a polynomial $P(x)$ is divided by $x-c$, the remainder is $P(c)$.
- 释 余式定理即一个多项式 $P(x)$ 除以 $x-c$，余数是 $P(c)$。

191 long division /dɪˈvɪʒn/   长除法

- 英 a method of dividing one number by another in which all the stages involved are written down
- 释 长除法是把一个数除以另一个数并把计算过程都写下来的方法。

192 partial /ˈpɑːʃl/ fraction /ˈfrækʃn/   部分分式

- 英 each of two or more fractions into which a more complex fraction can be decomposed as a sum
- 释 部分分式是一个复杂分数分解为两个或更多的分数之和的形式。

第二小节　Functions 函数

---

193 mapping /ˈmæpɪŋ/   n. 映射

- 英 a diagram to show how the numbers in the domain and range are paired
- 释 映射是表示定义域和范围内的数字如何成对的图表。

194 one-one function /ˈfʌŋkʃn/   一对一函数

- 英 a function where exactly one input value gives rise to each value in the range
- 释 在一对一函数中，每一个输入的值只有一个输出值映射在值域中。

195 many-one function — 多对一函数

- **E** a function which has one output value for each input value but each output value can have more than one input value
- **释** 在多对一函数中,每一个输入的值只有一个输出值映射在值域中,但输出值可以对应着多个输入值。

196 domain /dəˈmeɪn/ — *n.* 定义域

- **E** the set of input values for a function
- **释** 定义域即函数的输入值集。

197 range /reɪndʒ/ — *n.* 值域

- **E** the set of output values for a function
- **释** 值域即函数的输出值集。

198 self-inverse /ˌself ˌɪnˈvɜːs/ function — 反身函数

- **E** a function f where $f^{-1}(x) = f(x)$ for all x
- **释** 当 $f^{-1}(x) = f(x)$ 时,函数 $f(x)$ 被称为反身函数。

199 base /beɪs/ — *n.* 基数

- **E** When working with indices, the base is the number that is being raised to a power.
- **释** 基数是使用指数时被提升为幂的数字。

200 logarithm /ˈlɒɡərɪðəm/ — *n.* 对数

- **E** the power to which a base needs to be raised to produce a given value; For example, the logarithm of 100 to the base 10 is 2.
- **释** 一个数字的对数是必须产生另一个固定数字(基数)的指数。例如,以 10 为底的 100 的对数是 2。

201 natural logarithm — 自然对数

- **E** a logarithm to the base of e; $\ln x$ is used to represent $\log_e x$
- **释** 自然对数即以 e 为底的对数 $\ln x$,用来表示 $\log_e x$。

202 natural exponential /ˌekspəˈnenʃl/ function
自然指数函数

- **E** the function $y = e^x$
- **释** 自然指数函数即函数 $y = e^x$。

第三小节　Trigonometry 三角函数

203 radian /ˈreɪdiən/
n. 弧度

- **E** the angle subtended at the centre of a circle by an arc that is equal in length to the radius of a circle
- **释** 弧度是一个与圆的半径相等的弧对圆中心的角度。

204 quadrant /ˈkwɒdrənt/
n. 象限

- **E** The Cartesian plane is divided into four quadrants.
- **释** 笛卡尔平面划分为四个象限。
- **扩** first quadrant 第一象限

205 basic angle
基准角

- **E** the acute angle made with the x-axis
- **释** 基准角是与 x 轴形成的锐角。
- **同** reference angle

206 period /ˈpɪəriəd/
n. 周期

- **E** the length of one repetition or cycle of a periodic function
- **释** 周期是周期函数形成的一个重复或周期的长度。
- **扩** periodic function 周期函数
  - a function that repeats its values in regular intervals or periods
  - 周期函数是以一定的间隔或周期重复其值的函数。

207 **amplitude** /'æmplɪtjuːd/ *n.* 振幅

[E] the distance between a maximum (or minimum) point and the principal axis of a sinusoidal function

[释] 振幅是最大值（或最小值）点与正弦函数主轴之间的距离。

208 **principal** /'prɪnsəpl/ **angle** 主角

[E] the angle that the calculator gives

[释] 主角是计算器既定的角。

209 **identity** /aɪ'dentəti/ *n.* 恒等式

[E] a mathematical relationship equating one quantity to another

[释] 恒等式即把一个量等同于另一个量的数学关系。

210 **LHS (left-hand side)** *abbr.* 左手边

[E] LHS is informal shorthand for the left-hand side of an equation.

[释] LHS 是方程左手边的非正式缩写。

[扩] RHS (right-hand side) *abbr.* 右手边

- RHS is informal shorthand for the right-hand side of an equation.
- RHS 是方程右手边的非正式缩写。

211 **cosecant** /kəʊ'siːkənt/ *n.* 余割

[E] a trigonometric function θ that is the reciprocal of the sine for all real numbers θ for which the sine is not zero and that is exactly equal to the cosecant of an angle of measure θ in radians; i.e. $\operatorname{cosec}\theta=\dfrac{1}{\sin\theta}$.

[释] 三角函数 $\operatorname{cosec}\theta$ 是 $\sin\theta$（θ 为所有实数）的倒数，其正弦值不为零且等于弧度的测量角度 θ 的余割，即：$\operatorname{cosec}\theta=\dfrac{1}{\sin\theta}$。

212 **secant** /'siːkənt/ *n.* 正割

[E] a trigonometric function θ that is the reciprocal of the cosine for all real numbers θ for which the cosine is not, zero and that is exactly equal to the secant of an angle of measure θ in radians; i.e. $\sec \theta = \dfrac{1}{\cos \theta}$.

🅡 三角函数 $\sec \theta$ 是 $\cos \theta$（θ 为所有实数）的倒数，其余弦值不为零且等于弧度的测量角度 θ 的正割，即：$\sec \theta = \dfrac{1}{\cos \theta}$。

213 **cotangent** /kəʊ'tændʒənt/   *n.* 余切

🅔 a trigonometric function that is equal to the cosine divided by the sine for all real numbers for which the sine is not equal to zero and is exactly equal to the cotangent of an angle of measure in radians; i.e. $\cot \theta = \dfrac{1}{\tan \theta} = \dfrac{\cos \theta}{\sin \theta}$.

🅡 三角函数是 $\cos \theta$ 除以 $\sin \theta$（θ 为所有实数），其正弦值不为零且等于弧度的测量角度 θ 的余切，即：$\cot \theta = \dfrac{1}{\tan \theta} = \dfrac{\cos \theta}{\sin \theta}$。

214 **vertical** /'vɜːtɪkl/ **asymptote** /'æsɪmˌtəʊt/
垂直渐近线

🅔 vertical asymptotes are vertical lines near which the function grows without bound
🅡 垂直渐近线是函数在该垂线附近无限增长的垂直线。

215 **formula** /'fɔːmjələ/   *n.* 公式

🅔 a general 'rule' expressed algebraically
🅡 公式是用代数方法表示的一般"规则"。
🅟 formulae

216 **compound** /'kɒmpaʊnd/ **angle formulae** /'fɔːmjəliː/
复角公式

🅔 $\sin (A+B) = \sin A \cos B + \sin B \cos A$
$\sin (A−B) = \sin A \cos B − \sin B \cos A$
$\cos (A+B) = \cos A \cos B − \sin A \sin B$
$\cos (A−B) = \cos A \cos B + \sin A \sin B$

$\tan (A + B) = \dfrac{\tan A + \tan B}{1 - \tan A \tan B}$

$\tan (A + B) = \dfrac{\tan A - \tan B}{1 + \tan A \tan B}$

217 double angle formulae 倍角公式

- $\sin 2A = 2 \sin A \cos A$
- $\cos 2A = \cos^2 A - \sin^2 A$
- $\tan 2A = \dfrac{2 \tan A}{1 + \tan^2 A}$

扫一扫
听本节音频

第四小节 Series 级数

218 coefficient /ˌkəʊɪˈfɪʃnt/ *n.* 系数

- 🅔 a number which is placed before another quantity and which multiplies it; for example 3 in the quantity $3x$
- 🅡 系数是放在另一个数的前面并将其相乘的数，例如 $3x$ 中的 3 为系数。

219 binomial /baɪˈnəʊmiəl/ *n.* 二项式

- 🅔 an expression that has two groups of numbers or letters, joined by the sign + or -
- 🅡 二项式是由两组数字或字母组成，用符号 + 或 – 连接的表达式。
- 🅕 binomial coefficient 二项式系数
  - the coefficients in a binomial expansion
  - 二项式系数是二项展开式中的系数。

  binomial theorem 二项式定理
  - the rule for expanding $(1+x)n$ or $(a+b)n$
  - 二项式定理即把 $(1+x)n$ 或者 $(a+b)n$ 展开的方法。

220 Pascal's /ˈpæsˌkælz/ triangle
帕斯卡三角，杨辉三角

- 🅔 A triangular array of the binomial coefficients, where each number is the sum of the two numbers above.
- 🅡 帕斯卡三角是二项式系数的三角形阵列，其中每个数是上面两个数的和。

```
              1
            1   1
          1   2   1
        1   3   3   1
      1   4   6   4   1
    1   5  10  10   5   1
   ... ... ... ... ... ... ...
```

221 **factorial** /fæk'tɔːriəl/   *n.* 阶乘

- ☐ 🇪 The result when you multiply a whole number by all the numbers below it, e.g. 6!=1×2×3×4×5×6 (read as '6 factorial')
- ☐ 🇨 阶乘是所有小于及等于该数的正整数的积。例如，6!=1×2×3×4×5×6（读作"6 的阶乘"）

222 **arithmetic** /ə'rɪθmətɪk/ **progression** /prə'ɡreʃn/
等差数列

- ☐ 🇪 Each term in the progression differs from the term before by a constant.
- ☐ 🇨 等差数列是数列中的每一项与它的前一项的差等于同一个常数的一种数列。

223 **geometric** /ˌdʒiːə'metrɪk/ **progression** 等比数列

- ☐ 🇪 Each term in the progression is a constant multiple of the preceding term.
- ☐ 🇨 等比数列是数列中的每一项与它的前一项的倍数等于同一个常数的一种数列。

224 **common difference**   公差

- ☐ 🇪 The difference between successive terms in an arithmetic progression, usually written as d.
- ☐ 🇨 公差是等差数列中连续项之间的差，通常写为 d。

225 **common ratio**   公比

- ☐ 🇪 The constant ratio of successive terms in a geometric progression, usually written as r.
- ☐ 🇨 公比是等比数列中连续项的常数比，通常写为 r。

226 **converge** /kən'vɜːdʒ/ *vi.* 收敛

[E] to approach a limit as the number of terms increases without limit

[释] 收敛即无限增加项的数目直至接近极限。

[扩] convergent *adj.* 收敛的

- moving together from different directions and meeting
- 收敛的即从不同方向向一点靠近并汇聚在一起。

convergent series 收敛级数

- a sequence that tends to a finite number
- 收敛级数是不断趋向于给定数的序列。

第五小节 Differentiation and Differential Equation 微分和微分方程

扫一扫
听本节音频

227 **differentiation** /ˌdɪfəˌrenʃɪ'eɪʃn/ *n.* 微分

[E] the process of finding the gradient of a curve

[释] 微分是求曲线斜率的过程。

228 **derivative** /dɪ'rɪvətɪv/ *n.* 导数

[E] the result of mathematical differentiation; denoted by $\frac{dy}{dx}$

[释] 导数是数学微分的过程，记作 $\frac{dy}{dx}$。

229 **calculus** /'kælkjələs/ *n.* 微积分

[E] the branch of mathematics that is concerned with limits and with the differentiation and integration of functions

[释] 微积分是用于研究函数的极限、微分和积分的一个数学分支。

230 **chain rule** 链式法则

[E] the rule for computing the derivative of the composition of two functions

[释] 链式法则是计算两个函数复合导数的法则。

231 **normal** /ˈnɔːml/ *n.* 法线

- 🇪 the line perpendicular to the tangent at a point on a curve
- 🇨 法线是垂直于曲线上一点的切线的线。

232 **increasing function** 增函数

- 🇪 a function whose value increases as x increases
- 🇨 增函数即随着 x 的增加而增加的函数。
- 扩 decreasing function 减函数
  - a function whose value decreases as x increases
  - 减函数即随着 x 的增加而减少的函数。

233 **point of inflexion** /ɪnˈflekʃən/ 拐点

- 🇪 a point on a curve at which the direction of curvature changes
- 🇨 拐点即曲线上曲率方向发生变化的点。

234 **product rule** 乘积法则

- 🇪 In calculus, the product rule is a formula used to find the derivatives of products of two or more functions, i.e. $\dfrac{dy}{dx} = u\dfrac{dv}{dx} + \dfrac{du}{dx}v$.
- 🇨 在微分中,乘积法则是用来求两个或两个以上函数乘积的导数的公式,即: $\dfrac{dy}{dx} = u\dfrac{dv}{dx} + \dfrac{du}{dx}v$。

235 **quotient** /ˈkwəʊʃnt/ **rule** 除法法则

- 🇪 In calculus, the quotient rule is a method of finding the derivative of a function that is the quotient of two other functions for which derivatives exist, i.e. $\dfrac{dy}{dx} = \dfrac{vu' - uv'}{v^2}$.
- 🇨 在微分中,除法法则是一种求一个函数的导数的方法,该函数是另两个有导数的函数的商,即: $\dfrac{dy}{dx} = \dfrac{vu' - uv'}{v^2}$。

236 explicit /ɪkˈsplɪsɪt/ function   显函数

- **E** Functions of the form $y=f(x)$ are called explicit functions as y is given explicitly in terms of x.
- **释** 显函数是 y 以 x 的形式明显地给出，形如 $y=f(x)$ 的函数。
- **反** implicit function 隐函数
  - When a function is given as an equation connecting x and y, where y is not the subject.
  - 隐函数是给出为一个连接 x 和 y 的方程，但 y 不是方程式主体的函数。

237 parameter /pəˈræmɪtə(r)/   *n.* 参数

- **E** Sometimes variables x and y are given as a function of a third variable t. The variable t is called a parameter.
- **释** 有时变量 x 和 y 是第三个变量 t 的函数，这个变量 t 被称为参数。
- **扩** parametric equation 参数方程
  - Sometimes variables x and y are given as a function of a third variable t. The variable t is called a parameter and the two equations are called the parametric equations of the curve.
  - 有时变量 x 和 y 是第三个变量 t 的函数，变量 t 称为参数，这两个方程称为曲线的参数方程。

238 differential /ˌdɪfəˈrenʃl/ equations   微分方程

- **E** a mathematical equation that relates some function with its derivatives
- **释** 微分方程是将函数与其导数联系起来的数学方程。

239 general solution /səˈluːʃn/   通解

- **E** a solution for a differential equation that works for any value of the constant c
- **释** 通解是对任意常数 c 都成立的微分方程的解。

240 particular /pəˈtɪkjələ(r)/ solution   特解

- **E** a solution for a differential equation that works for a specific value of c
- **释** 特解是对特定的 c 值有效的微分方程的解。

241 **separation** /ˌsepəˈreɪʃn/   *n.* 分离

- 例 a method to solve the differential equation
- 释 分离是一种解微分方程的方法。

242 **arbitrary** /ˈɑːbɪtrəri/ **constant** /ˈkɒnstənt/
任意常数

- 例 a constant that may be assumed to be any value
- 释 任意常数是可假定为任意值的常数。

第六小节 Integration 积分

扫一扫
听本节音频

243 **integration** /ˌɪntɪˈɡreɪʃn/   *n.* 积分

- 例 the reverse process of differentiation
- 释 积分是与微分相反的过程。
- 同 antidifferentiation *n.* 逆微分

244 **integral** /ˈɪntɪɡrəl/   *n.* 积分

- 例 the result of a mathematical integration
- 释 积分是数学积分的结果。
- 扩 definite integral 定积分
  - an integral between limits whose result does not contain a constant of integration
  - 定积分是结果不包含积分常数的有限积分。

  indefinite integral 不定积分
  - an integral without limits whose result contains a constant of integration
  - 不定积分是结果包含一个积分常数的无限积分。

245 **improper integral**   **反常积分**

- 例 a definite integral that has either one limit or both limits are infinite, or a definite integral where the function to be integrated approaches an infinite value at either or both endpoints and the interval (of integration)

❷ 反常积分是具有一个极限或具有两个无限极限的定积分,或是积分函数在间隔(积分)的任一端点或两个端点处接近无限值的定积分。

246 **revolution** /ˌrevəˈluːʃn/   *n.* 旋转

- ❶ a circular movement made by something fixed to a central point
- ❷ 旋转是由固定在中心点上的物体所做的圆周运动。
- ❸ rotation
- ❹ solid of revolution 旋转体
  - the solid formed when an area is rotated through 360° about an axis
  - 旋转体是一个平面图形绕一个轴旋转360度时形成的立体图形。

  volume of revolution 旋转体的体积
  - the volume of the solid formed when an area is rotated through 360° about an axis
  - 旋转体的体积是一个平面图形绕一个轴旋转360度时形成的立体图形的体积。

247 **trapezium** /trəˈpiːziəm/ **rule**   梯形法则

- ❶ a technique for approximating the definite integral
- ❷ 梯形法则是一种近似定积分的法则。

248 **overestimate** /ˌəʊvərˈestɪmeɪt/   *vi.* 高估

- ❶ to estimate something to be larger, better, etc. than it really is
- ❷ 高估即估计某事比实际情况更大、更好等。
- ❸ underestimate *vi.* 低估
  - to estimate something to be lower, smaller, etc. than it really is
  - 低估即估计某物比实际值低、小等。

249 **concave** /kɒnˈkeɪv/   *adj.* 凹面的

- ❶ meaning curving in or hollowed inward
- ❷ 凹面的即向内弯曲或向内凹的。
- ❸ convex *adj.* 凸面的
  - meaning curving out or extending outward
  - 凸面的即向外弯曲或向外延伸的。

250 **integration** /ˌɪntɪˈɡreɪʃn/ **by substitution** /ˌsʌbstɪˈtjuːʃən/ 换元积分法

- ☒ **E** can be considered as the reverse process of differentiation by the chain rule
- ☒ **释** 换元积分法是用链式法则求微分的逆过程。

251 **integration by parts** 分步积分法

- ☒ **E** a theorem that relates the integral of a product of functions to the integral of their derivative and antiderivative; i.e. $\int u \dfrac{dv}{dx} dx = uv - \int v \dfrac{du}{dx} dx$.
- ☒ **释** 分步积分法是一个将函数乘积的积分与它们的导数和不定积分联系起来的定理,即:$\int u \dfrac{dv}{dx} dx = uv - \int v \dfrac{du}{dx} dx$。

第七小节　Numerical Solution and Vectors 数值解和向量

扫一扫
听本节音频

252 **iteration** /ˌɪtəˈreɪʃn/ *n.* 迭代

- ☒ **E** one trial in a process that is repeated such as when using an iterative formula (see iterative process)
- ☒ **释** 迭代是使用迭代公式(参见迭代过程)重复计算的方法。
- **扩** iterative formula 迭代公式
  - the type of formula that is used repeatedly; The output from each stage is used as the input for the next stage. It is commonly used in numerical methods.
  - 迭代公式是重复使用的一种公式。它每个阶段的输出用作下一阶段的输入,通常用于数值方法中。

iterative process 迭代过程
  - a process for finding a particular result by repeating trials of operations; Each repeat trial is called an iteration and each iteration should produce a value closer to the result being found.
  - 迭代过程即通过重复操作试验来找到特定结果的过程。每个重复试验称为一个迭代,每个迭代应该产生一个更接近结果的值。

253 resultant /rɪˈzʌltənt/ vector /ˈvektə(r)/ 合成向量

[E] the combination of two or more single vectors

[释] 合成向量是两个或多个单向量的组合。

254 vector addition /əˈdɪʃn/ 向量加法

[E] the process of finding the sum of two or more vectors

[释] 向量加法是求两个或多个向量的和的过程。

[反] vector subtraction 向量减法

- the addition of the negative of a vector
- 向量减法是向量的负数相加。

255 commutative /kəˈmjuːtətɪv/ *adj.* 交换的

[E] giving the same result whatever the order in which the quantities are shown; i.e. $a+b=b+a$.

[释] 交换的即无论数量的顺序如何，其计算结果不变，即：$a+b=b+a$。

256 magnitude /ˈmægnɪtjuːd/ *n.* 大小

[E] the property of relative size or extent (whether large or small)

[释] 大小即比较尺寸或范围的性质（或大或小）。

[扩] magnitude of a vector 向量的大小

- the length or size of the vector
- 向量的大小即向量的长度或尺寸。

257 unit vector 单位向量

[E] a vector with magnitude or length one

[释] 单位向量是大小或长度为 1 的向量。

258 scalar /ˈskeɪlə(r)/ product 点积

[E] the product of two vectors to form a scalar, whose value is the product of the magnitudes of the vectors and the cosine of the angle between them

[释] 点积即两个向量的乘积形成的一个标量，它的值等于两个向量的大小和它们之间夹角的余弦值的乘积。

[同] dot product

259 **skew** /skjuː/   *adj.* 歪斜的；异面的

- ☐ ☐ ☐ 🅔 Skew lines are two lines that do not intersect and are not parallel.
- 🈩 斜直线即两条直线异面既不相交也不平行。

第八小节　Complex Numbers 复数

260 **complex** /ˈkɒmpleks/ **number**   复数

- ☐ ☐ ☐ 🅔 a number that can be written in the form $x+iy$ where x and y are real; This form of a complex number is called the Cartesian form.
- 🈩 复数是一个可以写为 $x+iy$ 形式的数（x 和 y 为实数）。复数的这种形式叫作笛卡儿形式。

261 **imaginary** /ɪˈmædʒɪnəri/ **number**   虚数

- ☐ ☐ ☐ 🅔 any multiple of the unit imaginary number i where i^2 is defined to be -1
- 🈩 虚数即 i（规定 i^2=-1），可与实数进行四则运算。

262 **complex conjugate** /ˈkɒndʒəgeɪt/   共轭复数

- 🅔 the complex number whose imaginary part is the negative of that of a given complex number, the real parts of both numbers being equal; e.g. The complex conjugate of $z=x+yi$ is defined as $z^*=x-yi$.
- 🈩 两个实部相等，虚部互为相反数的复数互为共轭复数，例如，$z=x+yi$ 的复共轭定义为 $z^*=x-yi$。
- 🈷 conjugate pair 共轭对
  - $x+yi$ and $x-yi$ are conjugate pair.
  - $x+yi$ 和 $x-yi$ 是共轭对。

263 Argand diagram /ˈdaɪəɡræm/ 阿根图

E a diagram in which complex numbers are represented by the points in the plane the coordinates of which are respectively the real and imaginary parts of the number; The number $x+yi$ is represented by the point (x, y).

释 阿根图是用平面上的点表示复数的图表，这些点的坐标分别是数字的实部和虚部，数字 $x+yi$ 由点 (x, y) 表示。

264 modulus /ˈmɒdjʊləs/ n. 模

E The modulus of the complex number $x+yi$ is the magnitude of the position vector $\begin{pmatrix} x \\ y \end{pmatrix}$.

释 复数 $x+yi$ 的模是位置矢量 $\begin{pmatrix} x \\ y \end{pmatrix}$ 的大小。

265 argument /ˈɑːɡjumənt/ n. 辐角

E The argument of a complex number $x+yi$ is the direction of the position vector $\begin{pmatrix} x \\ y \end{pmatrix}$.

释 复数 $x+yi$ 的辐角是位置矢量 $\begin{pmatrix} x \\ y \end{pmatrix}$ 的方向。

266 Cartesian /kɑːˈtɪːziən/ form 笛卡尔形式

E $z = x + yi$ is the Cartesian form for a complex number.

释 $z = x + yi$ 是复数的笛卡尔形式。

267 modulus-argument form 复数的模-幅角形式

E $z = r(\cos\theta + i\sin\theta)$ is the modulus-argument form for a complex number.

释 $z = r(\cos\theta + i\sin\theta)$ 是复数的模 – 幅角形式。

268 exponential /ˌekspəˈnenʃl/ form 指数形式

E $z = re^{i\theta}$ is the exponential form for a complex number.

释 $z = re^{i\theta}$ 是复数的指数形式。

269 polar /ˈpəʊlə(r)/ coordinate /kəʊˈɔːdɪnət/ 极坐标

E The polar coordinate is a two-dimensional coordinate system in which each point on a plane is determined by a distance from a fixed point and an angle from a fixed direction, written as (r, θ).

释 极坐标是一个二维坐标系，平面上的每个点都由与固定点的距离和与固定方向的角度决定，写为 (r, θ).。

270 polar form 极坐标形式

E the modulus-argument and exponential forms of a complex number are polar forms

释 复数的模–幅角形式和指数形式是极坐标形式。

271 cubic /ˈkjuːbɪk/ equation 三次方程

E a cubic function defined by a polynomial of degree three

释 三次方程是未知数最高次数为三次的多项式方程。

272 quartic /ˈkwɔːtɪk/ equation 四次方程

E a quartic function defined by a polynomial of degree four

释 四次方程是未知数最高次数为四次的多项式方程。

273 square root 平方根

E a number which, when multiplied by itself produces a particular number; e.g. The square root of 64 is ± 8.

释 一个数与自身相乘得到另一个特定数，这个数即为这个特定数的平方根，例如，64 的平方根是 ± 8。

274 cube root 立方根

E a number which, when multiplied by itself twice, produces a particular number; e.g. The cube root of 64 is 4.

释 一个数与自身相乘两次得到一个特定的数，这个数即为这个特定数的立方根，例如，64 的立方根是 4。

275 unity /'juːnəti/ n. 一

[E] the number one

[释] 一即数字一。

276 locus /'ləʊkəs/ n. 轨迹

[E] a path traced out by a point as it moves following a particular rule; The rule is expressed as an inequality or an equation.

[释] 轨迹是一个点沿着特定的规则运动时所描绘出的轨迹。这个规则可表示为不等式或方程。

[复] loci

277 half line 射线

[E] a straight line extending from a point

[释] 射线是从一点延伸出来的直线。

第九小节 Pre-calculus 初级微积分 ★（仅 AP 掌握）

扫一扫
听本节音频

278 continuous /kən'tɪnjuəs/ function 连续函数

[E] a function for which small changes in the input result in small changes in the output

[释] 连续函数是一种输入的微小变化导致输出的微小变化的函数。

[反] discontinuous function 不连续函数

279 even function 偶函数

[E] a function which satisfies particular symmetry relations, with respect to taking additive inverses; i.e. $f(x)=f(-x)$

[释] 偶函数是在加法逆运算中满足特定对称关系的函数，例如，$f(x)=f(-x)$。

280 odd function 奇函数

- 🇬🇧 a function which satisfies particular symmetry relations; with respect to taking additive inverses, i.e. $-f(x) = f(-x)$
- 🇨🇳 奇函数是在加法逆运算中满足特定对称关系的函数，例如，$-f(x) = f(-x)$。

281 Squeeze Theorem 夹挤定理

- 🇬🇧 a theorem regarding the limit of a function
- 🇨🇳 夹挤定理是有关函数极限的定理。
- 📖 Sandwich Theorem 三明治定理

282 infinite /ˈɪnfɪnət/ function 界函数

- 🇬🇧 The function $f(x)$ is said to become infinite (positively or negatively) as x approaches c if $f(x)$ can be made arbitrarily large (positively or negatively) by taking x sufficiently close to c.
- 🇨🇳 界函数是指如果通过使 x 足够接近 c 可以使 $f(x)$ 任意大（正或负），则函数 $f(x)$ 会随着 x 接近 c 而变得无限大（正向或负向）。

283 intermediate /ˌɪntəˈmiːdiət/ value theorem /ˈθɪərəm/ 介值定理

- 🇬🇧 The intermediate value theorem states that if a continuous function f with an interval [a, b] as its domain takes values $f(a)$ and $f(b)$ at each end of the interval, then it also takes any value between $f(a)$ and $f(b)$ at some point within the interval.
- 🇨🇳 介值定理指出，如果以区间 [a, b] 为域的连续函数 f 在区间的两端都取值 $f(a)$ 和 $f(b)$，那么它在 $f(a)$ 和 $f(b)$ 之间取的任何值都在区间 [a, b] 内。

284 discontinuity /ˌdɪskɒntɪˈnjuːəti/ n. 不连续性

- 🇬🇧 the state of not being continuous
- 🇨🇳 不连续性即不能连续的状态。
- 📖 discrete *adj.* 分离的；互不相连的

- **infinite discontinuity** 无穷不连续
  - Whenever the graph of a function $f(x)$ has the line $x=a$ as a vertical asymptote, then $f(x)$ becomes positively or negatively infinite as $x \to a+$ or as $x \to a-$. The function is then said to have an infinite discontinuity.
  - 每当函数 $f(x)$ 的图形具有 $x=a$ 线作为垂直渐近线时，$f(x)$ 就会以 $x \to a+$ 或 $x \to a-$ 变为正或负无穷大，则该函数具有无穷不连续性。

  jump discontinuity 跳跃不连续
  - Where the left- and right-hand limits exist, but are different, the function has a jump discontinuity.
  - 如果存在左、右极限，但它们不同，则函数具有跳跃不连续性。

  removable discontinuity 可移不连续
  - a point at which a graph is not connected but can be made connected by filling in a single point.
  - 可移不连续是指一个图形没有被连接，但可以通过填充单个点使其连接的点。

第十小节　Calculus 微积分 ★（仅 AP 掌握）

285 **continuity** /ˌkɒntɪˈnjuːəti/　　　*n.* 连续的

- **E** the fact of not stopping or not changing
- **释** 连续的即恒定不变的事实。

286 **slope** /sləʊp/ **field**　　　斜率场

- **E** a graphical representation of the solutions of a first-order differential equation.
- **释** 斜率场是一阶微分方程解的图示。

287 **half-life** /ˈhɑːf laɪf/　　　*n.* 半衰期

- **E** the time taken for the radioactivity of a substance to fall to half its original value
- **释** 半衰期即一种物质的放射性下降到其原有值的一半所需要的时间。

288 mean value theorem 中值定理

🇪 The mean value theorem states, that given a planar arc between two endpoints, there is at least one point at which the tangent to the arc is parallel to the secant through its endpoints.

🇨 中值定理即给定两个端点之间的平面弧,在至少一个点处,弧的切线通过其端点平行于割线。

289 motion /ˈməʊʃn/ *n.* 动作

🇪 the act or process of moving or the way something moves

🇨 动作是移动的动作、过程或某事物的移动方式。

290 Rolle's theorem 罗尔定理

🇪 Rolle's theorem essentially states that any real-valued differentiable function that attains equal values at two distinct points must have a stationary point somewhere between them, that is, a point where the first derivative is zero.

🇨 罗尔定理即在两个不同的点上获得相等值的任何实值可微函数必须在它们之间的某个位置有一个稳定点(拐点),即一阶导数为零的点。

291 fundamental /ˌfʌndəˈmentl/ theorem of calculus /ˈkælkjələs/ 微积分基本定理

🇪 a theorem that links the concept of the derivative of a function with the concept of the integral

🇨 微积分基本定理是将函数导数的概念与积分的概念联系起来的定理。

292 Riemann /riːmɑːn/ sum 黎曼和

🇪 an approximation of the area of a region, often the region underneath a curve

🇨 黎曼和是一个区域面积的近似值,通常是曲线下方的区域。

293 **trapezoid** /ˈtræpəzɔɪd/ **rule** 梯形法则

[E] a technique for approximating the definite integral

[释] 梯形法则是一种近似定积分的法则。

[同] trapezium rule

★仅 BC 掌握

294 **L'Hôpital's rule** 洛必达法则

[E] using derivatives to help evaluate limits involving indeterminate forms

[释] 洛必达法则即使用导数来计算不定式的极限。

295 **Euler's** /ˈɔllər/ **Method** 欧拉方法

[E] can solve first order first degree differential equation with a given initial value

[释] 欧拉方法可求解给定初值的一阶微分方程。

296 **indeterminate** /ˌɪndiˈtɜːmɪnət/ **form** 不定式

[E] an algebraic expression obtained in the context of limits; The most common indeterminate forms are denoted $\frac{0}{0}, \frac{\infty}{\infty}, 0\times\infty, 0^0, \infty^0$, etc.

[释] 不定式是在极限情况下获得的代数表达式。最常见的不定式表示为$\frac{0}{0}$，$\frac{\infty}{\infty}$，$0\times\infty$，0^0，∞^0等。

第十一小节 Application 应用★（仅 AP 掌握）

扫一扫
听本节音频

297 **absolute** /ˈæbsəluːt/ **maximum** /ˈmæksɪməm/ 绝对最大值

[E] The absolute maximum of a function on $[a, b]$ occurs at $x = c$ if $f(c) \geq f(x)$ for all x on $[a, b]$.

[释] 如果 $[a, b]$ 上所有 x 的 $f(c) \geq f(x)$，则 $[a, b]$ 上的函数的绝对最大值出现在 $x = c$ 处。

[同] global maximum 全局最大值

298 **absolute minimum** /ˈmɪnɪməm/ 绝对最小值

[E] The absolute minimum of a function on $[a, b]$ occurs at x=c if $f(c) \leq f(x)$ for all x on $[a, b]$.

[释] 如果 $[a, b]$ 上所有 x 的 $f(c) \leq f(x)$，则 $[a, b]$ 上的函数的绝对最小值出现在 $x=c$ 处。

[同] global minimum 全局最小值

299 **concavity** /kɒnˈkævəti/ *n.* 凹面

[E] the quality of being concave

[释] 凹面即凹入的性质。

[反] convexity *n.* 凸面

- the quality of being convex
- 凸面即凸出的性质。

300 **disk** /dɪsk/ *n.* 磁盘

[E] a device for storing information on a computer, with a magnetic surface that records information received in electronic form

[释] 磁盘是一种在计算机上存储信息的装置，其磁表面以电子形式记录接收到的信息。

301 linearisation /ˌlɪnɪəraɪˈzeɪʃən/   *n.* 线性化

- **例** In mathematics linearisation refers to finding the linear approximation to a function at a given point.
- **释** 在数学中,线性化是指在给定点上找到函数的线性近似。

302 net accumulation /əˌkjuːmjəˈleɪʃn/   积累净额

- **例** The definite integral of the rate of change of a quantity over an interval is the net accumulation of the quantity over that interval.
- **释** 一个量在一个区间内的变化率的定积分是这个量在这个区间内的积累净额。

303 net change   净变化

- **例** $F(b)-F(a)$ is the net change in $F(t)$ as t varies from a to b.
- **释** $F(b)-F(a)$ 是 t 从 a 到 b 变化时 $F(t)$ 的净变化。

304 optimisation /ˌɒptɪmaɪˈzeɪʃn/   *n.* 最优化

- **例** Mathematical optimisation is the selection of a best element from some set of available alternatives.
- **释** 数学的最优化是从一组可用的备选方案中选择最佳方案。

305 shell /ʃel/   *n.* 壳

- **例** In geometry, a spherical shell is a generalisation of an annulus to three dimensions. It is the region between two concentric spheres of differing radii.
- **释** 在几何学上,球壳是立体环状结构,是两个半径不同的同心球体之间的区域。

306 washer /ˈwɒʃə(r)/   *n.* 垫圈

- **例** a disk with a hole in it
- **释** 垫圈是有孔的圆盘。

★ 仅 BC 掌握

307 comparison /kəm'pærɪsn/ test 比较检验

- **E** a method of testing for the convergence of an infinite series
- **释** 比较检验是一种检验无穷级数收敛性的方法。

第十二小节 Sequences and Series
数列和级数 ★（仅 BC 掌握）

308 absolute convergence /kən'vɜːdʒəns/ 绝对收敛

- **E** An infinite series of numbers is said to converge absolutely if the sum of the absolute values of the summands is finite.
- **释** 如果一个无穷级数的和的绝对值的和是有限的，那么这个数列就是绝对收敛。

309 conditional /kən'dɪʃnl/ convergence 条件收敛

- **E** A series or integral is said to be conditionally convergent if it converges, but it does not converge absolutely.
- **释** 如果一个数列或一个整数积分收敛，则是条件收敛，但它不是绝对收敛。

310 alternating /'ɔːltəneɪtɪŋ/ series 交错级数

- **E** an infinite series of the form $\sum_{n=0}^{\infty}(-1)^n a_n$ or $\sum_{n=0}^{\infty}(-1)^{n+1} a_n$ with $a_n>0$ for all n; The signs of the general terms alternate between positive and negative.
- **释** 交错级数是形式为 $\sum_{n=0}^{\infty}(-1)^n a_n$ 或 $\sum_{n=0}^{\infty}(-1)^{n+1} a_n$（$a>0$）的无穷级数。一般术语的符号在正负之间交替。

311 convergent sequence /ˈsiːkwəns/ 收敛数列

- The limit of a sequence is the value that the terms of a sequence 'tend to'. If such a limit exists, the sequence is called convergent.
- 数列的极限是数列项"趋向"的值。如果存在这样的极限，则数列称为收敛数列。

312 convergent series 收敛级数

- A series is convergent if the sequence of its partial sums tends to a limit.
- 数列所对应的值无限趋向于极限时，这个级数则为收敛级数。

313 divergent /daɪˈvɜːdʒənt/ series 发散级数

- an infinite series that is not convergent, meaning that the infinite sequence of the partial sums of the series does not have a finite limit
- 发散级数是一个级数的部分和的无穷序列没有限制的非收敛的无穷级数。

314 Euler's formula /ˈfɔːmjələ/ 欧拉公式

- a mathematical formula in complex analysis that establishes the deep relationship between the trigonometric functions and the complex exponential function; i.e. $e^{i\pi}+1=0$.
- 欧拉公式是复杂分析三角函数与复杂指数函数之间的深层关系的数学公式，即：$e^{i\pi}+1=0$。

315 harmonic /hɑːˈmɒnɪk/ series /ˈsɪəriːz/ 调和级数

- the divergent infinite series, $\sum_{n=0}^{\infty}\frac{1}{n}=1+\frac{1}{2}+\frac{1}{3}+\frac{1}{4}+\ldots$
- 调和级数是发散的无穷级数，即：$\sum_{n=0}^{\infty}\frac{1}{n}=1+\frac{1}{2}+\frac{1}{3}+\frac{1}{4}+\cdots\cdots$。

316 Taylor series 泰勒级数

- **E** a representation of a function as an infinite sum of terms that are calculated from the values of the function's derivatives at a single point
- **释** 泰勒级数是函数的无穷项之和,由单点函数的导数值计算得出。
- **扩** Maclaurin series 麦克劳林级数
  - If the Taylor series is centered at zero, then that series is called a Maclaurin series.
  - 函数在 x=0 处的泰勒级数称为麦克劳林级数。

317 Taylor's theorem 泰勒定理

- **E** giving an approximation of a k times differentiable function around a given point by a kth order Taylor polynomial
- **释** 泰勒定理是一个用 k 阶泰勒多项式取定点附近的 k 次微分函数的近似值的公式。

第二节

Statistics 统计

扫一扫
听本节音频

第一小节 Representation of Data 数据表示

318 qualitative /'kwɒlɪtətɪv/ **data** 定性数据

[E] data that take non-numerical values; e.g. colour

[释] 定性数据是带有非数值的数据，例如，颜色。

[同] categorical data 分类数据

[易] quantitative data 定量数据

- data that take numerical values; e.g. number of people
- 定量数据是带有数值的数据，例如，人数。

319 raw /rɔː/ **data** 原始数据

[E] numerical facts and other pieces of information in their original form

[释] 原始数据是数字事实和其他原始形式的信息。

320 lower boundary /'baʊndri/ 下限

[E] the smallest values that can exist in a class of continuous data

[释] 下限是一类连续数据中可以存在的最小值。

321 upper boundary 上限

[E] the largest values that can exist in a class of continuous data

[释] 上限是一类连续数据中可以存在的最大值。

322 class width /wɪdθ/ 组宽

[E] the difference between the upper boundary and the lower boundary of a class

[释] 组宽是一组的上限和下限之间的差。

323 **class interval** /'ɪntəvl/ 组距

- **E** the range of values from the lower boundary to the upper boundary of a class
- **释** 组距是一组的下限到上限的范围。

324 **class mid-value** 组中值

- **E** the value exactly half-way between the lower boundary and the upper boundary of a class
- **释** 组中值是恰好位于类的下边界和上边界之间的中间位置的值。
- **同** mid-point

325 **grouped frequency** /'fri:kwənsi/ **table**
分组频率表

- **E** a frequency table in which values are grouped into classes
- **释** 分组频率表是所有值被分到不同组中的频率表。

326 **cumulative** /'kju:mjələtɪv/ **frequency graph**
累积频数图

- **E** a graphical representation of the number of readings below a given value made by plotting cumulative frequencies against upper class boundaries for all intervals
- **释** 累积频数图是通过绘制已给的频率累加来表示给定值读数的图表。

327 **average** /'æverɪdʒ/ *n.* 平均,平均数

- **E** any of the measures of central tendency, including the mean, median and mode
- **释** 平均数是表示一组数据集中趋势的量数,包括平均值、中位数和众数。
- **同** mean

328 **summarise** /ˈsʌməraɪz/   *vt.* 概括

- **E** to give an accurate general description
- **释** 概括即给出准确的一般描述。

329 **coded** /ˈkəʊdɪd/   *adj.* 编码的

- **E** adjusted throughout by the same amount and/or by the same factor
- **释** 编码的即按相同数量和／或相同因素调配的。

330 **outlier** /ˈaʊtlaɪə(r)/   *n.* 异常值

- **E** an observation that lies an abnormal distance from other values in a set of data
- **释** 异常值是与一组数据中的其他值存在异常距离的观察值。
- **同** extreme value 极值

331 **skewed** /skjuːd/   *adj.* 歪斜的

- **E** unsymmetrical
- **释** 歪斜的即不对称的。

332 **variation** /ˌveərɪˈeɪʃn/   *n.* 变化

- **E** a measure of how widely spread out a set of data values is
- **释** 变化是测量一组数据值的分布范围。
- **同** dispersion

333 **standard deviation** /ˌdiːvɪˈeɪʃn/   标准差

- **E** a measure of spread based on how far the data values are from the mean; the square root of the variance.
- **释** 标准差是一种基于数据值离均值有多远的差值量数，即方差的平方根。

334 **variance** /ˈveərɪəns/   *n.* 方差

- **E** the mean squared deviation from the mean; the square of the standard deviation
- **释** 方差是离均值的平方偏差或标准差的平方。

第二小节　Probability, Permutations and Combinations 概率、排列和组合

扫一扫
听本节音频

335 **elementary** /ˌelɪˈmentri/ **event**   基本事件

- **E** an outcome of an experiment
- **释** 基本事件即实验的结果。

336 **favourable** /ˈfeɪvərəbl/   *adj.* 有利的，顺利的

- **E** leading to the occurrence of a required event
- **释** 有利的即导致必需事件的发生。

337 **random** /ˈrændəm/   *adj.* 随机的

- **E** occurring by chance and without bias
- **释** 随机的即不带有主观意见、偶然发生的。

338 **equiprobable** /ˌikwəˈprɑbəbəl/   *adj.* 等概率的

- **E** (events or outcomes that are) equally likely to occur
- **释** 等概率的即同样可能发生的（事件或结果）。

339 **relative frequency**   相对频率

- **E** the proportion of trials in which a particular event occurs
- **释** 相对频率是实验中某个特定事件出现的次数比例。

340 **expectation** /ˌekspekˈteɪʃn/   *n.* 期望值，预期

- **E** the expected number of times an event occurs
- **释** 期望值是事件发生的预期次数。

341 **selection** /sɪˈlekʃn/   *n.* 选择

- ☒ an item or number of items that are chosen
- ㊗ 选择是所选项目或项目数。
- 扩 combination *n.* 组合
  - the different selections that can be made from a set of objects
  - 组合即从一组对象中进行的不同的选择。

342 **arrangement** /əˈreɪndʒmənt/   *n.* 布置，整理

- ☒ a group of things that are organised or placed in a particular order or position
- ㊗ 布置即一组以特定顺序或位置组织或放置的事物。
- 扩 permutation *n.* 排列
  - the different orders in which objects can be selected and placed
  - 排列即可以选择、放置事物的不同的顺序。

第三小节　Distributions 分布

扫一扫
听本节音频

343 **probability** /ˌprɒbəˈbɪləti/ **distribution** /ˌdɪstrɪˈbjuːʃn/   概率分布

- ☒ a display of all the possible values of a variable and their corresponding probabilities
- ㊗ 概率分布是显示变量的所有可能值及其相应的概率。

344 **mathematical** /ˌmæθəˈmætɪkl/ **model**   数学模型

- ☒ a description of a system using mathematical concepts and language
- ㊗ 数学模型是用来描述数学概念和语言的系统。

345 **binomial** /baɪˈnəʊmiəl/ **distribution**   二项分布

- ☒ a discrete probability distribution of the possible number of successful outcomes in a finite number of independent trials, where the probability of success in each trial is the same
- ㊗ 二项分布是在有限数目的独立试验中表示可能成功数目的离散概率分布，其中每项试验成功的概率是相同的。

346 **geometric** /ˌdʒiːəˈmetrɪk/ **distribution**　几何分布

- **E** a discrete probability distribution of the possible number of trials required to obtain the first successful outcome in an infinite number of independent trials, where the probability of success in each trial is the same
- **释** 几何分布是获得无限数量的独立试验中首次成功所需的可能试验次数的离散概率分布，其中每个试验中的成功概率相同。

347 **normal distribution**　正态分布

- **E** a function that represents the probability distribution of particular continuous random variables as a symmetrical bell-shaped graph
- **释** 正态分布是指将特定连续随机变量的概率分布表示为对称钟形图的函数。

348 **probability density** /ˈdensəti/ **function (PDF)**　概率密度分布函数

- **E** a graph illustrating the probabilities for values of a continuous random variable
- **释** 概率密度分布函数即描述连续随机变量值的概率的图表。

349 **normal curve**　正态曲线

- **E** a symmetrical, bell-shaped curve
- **释** 正态曲线是对称的钟形曲线。

350 **standard normal variable** /ˈveəriəbl/　标准正态变量

- **E** the normally distributed variable, Z, with mean 0 and variance 1
- **释** 标准正态变量是正态分布变量，Z 的均值为 0，方差为 1。

第四小节　Exploring Data 探索数据
★（仅 AP 掌握）

扫一扫
听本节音频

351　**categorical** /ˌkætəˈɡɒrɪkl/ **variable**　分类变量

- variable that places an individual into one of several groups or categories
- 分类变量是将单一分类数据置于多组或多类别的变量。

352　**quantitative** /ˈkwɒntɪtətɪv/ **variable**　定量变量

- variable that takes numerical values for which it makes sense to find an average
- 定量变量是一种采用具有合理意义的数值以寻找平均值的变量。

353　**one-way table**　单向表

- table used to display the distribution of a single categorical variable
- 单向表是用于显示单个类别变量的分布的表。

354　**two-way table**　双向表

- table of counts that organises data about two categorical variables
- 双向表是一种用于组织有关两个类别变量数据的计数表。

355　**marginal** /ˈmɑːdʒɪnl/ **distribution**　边际分布

- the distribution of one of the categorical variables in a two-way table of counts among all individuals described by the table
- 边际分布是指在一个双向计数表中所描述的所有个体的分类变量的分布。

356 conditional /kənˈdɪʃənl/ distribution 条件分布

英 term that describes the values of one variable among individuals who have a specific value of another variable; There is a separate conditional distribution for each value of the other variable.

释 条件分布即一个变量在具有另一个变量特定值的个体之间的值，其他变量的每个值都有单独的条件分布。

357 side-by-side bar graph 并排条形图

英 graph used to compare the distribution of a categorical variable in each of several groups; For each value of the categorical variable, there is a bar corresponding to each group. The height of each bar is determined by the count or percent of individuals in the group with that value.

释 并排条形图是用于比较几类中每个类别的分类变量分布的图。分类变量的每个值都有一个对应于每个组的条形图。每个条形图的高度取决于该值在该组中的人数或百分比。

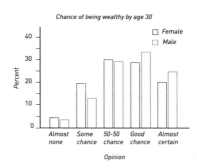

358 segmented /ˈsegmentɪd/ bar graph 分段条形图

英 graph used to compare the distribution of a categorical variable in each of several groups; For each group, there is a single bar with 'segments' that correspond to the different values of the categorical variable. The height of each segment is determined by the percent of individuals in the group with

that value. Each bar has a total height of 100%.
- 释 分段条形图是用于比较几组中每个类别变量的分布的图。每个组都有一个带有"段"的栏，分别对应于分类变量的不同值。每个段的高度由该值在组中各类的百分比确定，每个条的总高度为100%。

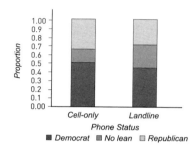

359 **association** /əˌsəʊsiˈeɪʃn/   n. 关联

- E knowing the value of one variable helps predict the value of the other; If knowing the value of one variable does not help predict the value of the other, there is no association between the variables.
- 释 通过一个变量的值可以帮助预测另一个变量的值，则这两个变量关联。如果知道一个变量的值不能帮助预测另一个变量的值，则变量之间没有关联。
- 同 correlation

360 **variability** /ˌveəriəˈbɪləti/ **of statistic** /stəˈtɪstɪk/
统计数据的差异性

- E spread of a statistics' sampling distribution; Statistics from larger samples have less variability.
- 释 统计数据的差异性即统计数据抽样分布的零散状况。来自较大样本的统计数据的差异性较小。

361 **five-number summary** /ˈsʌməri/ 五数概括法

- **E** smallest observation, first quartile, median, third quartile, and largest observation, written in order from smallest to largest; In symbols: Minimum, Q1, Median, Q3, Maximum.
- **释** 五数概括法即用下面的五个数来概括数据，将数据按递增顺序排列：最小值、第 1 四分位数（Q1）、中位数（Q2）、第 3 四分位数（Q3）、最大值。

362 **resistant** /rɪˈzɪstənt/ **measure** 抗测量

- **E** statistic that is not affected very much by extreme observations
- **释** 抗测量即受极端观测影响不大的统计数据。

第五小节　Modeling Distribution of Data
数据分布建模 ★（仅 AP 掌握）

---

363 **cumulative** /ˈkjuːmjələtɪv/ **relative frequency graph** 累积相对频率图

- **E** graph used to examine location within a distribution; Cumulative relative frequency graphs begin by grouping the observations into equal-width classes. The completed graph shows the accumulating percent of observations as you move through the classes in increasing order.
- **释** 累积相对频率图是用于检查分布位置的图。累积相对频率图首先将观测结果分组到等宽类中，并完整按递增顺序显示了遍历各个类时观察值的累计百分比。

364 **density curve** 密度曲线

- **E** curve that (a) is always on or above the horizontal axis and (b) has area exactly 1 underneath it; A density curve describes the overall pattern of a distribution. The area under the curve and above any interval of values on the horizontal axis is the proportion of all observations that fall in that interval.

释 密度曲线即（a）始终在水平轴上或水平轴上方且（b）在其正下方的面积恰好为1的曲线。密度曲线描述了分布的总体模式。曲线下方和水平轴上任何值区间上方的区域是该区间内所有观测值的比例。

365 **68-95-99.7 rule** 68-95-99.7 法则

- 英 In the normal distribution with mean *m* and standard deviation *s*, (a) approximately 68% of the observations fall within *s* of the mean *m*, (b) approximately 95% of the observations fall within 2s of *m*, and (c) approximately 99.7% of the observations fall within 3s of *m*.
- 释 68-85-99.7 法则即在均值为 m 和标准差为 s 的正态分布中，（a）大约 68% 的观测值落在均值 m±s 内，（b）大约 95% 的观测值落入均值 m±2s 内，并且（c）大约 99.7% 的观测值位于 m±3s 之内。
- 同 empirical rule 经验法则

第六小节 Describing Relationship 关系描述 ★（仅 AP 掌握）

扫一扫
听本节音频

366 **scatterplot** /ˌskætəˈplɒt/ *n.* 散点图

- 英 plot that shows the relationship between two quantitative variables measured on the same individuals; The values of one variable appear on the horizontal axis, and the values of the other variable appear on the vertical axis. Each individual in the data appears as a point in the graph.
- 释 散点图是表示在相同个体上测量的两个定量变量之间关系的图。一个变量的值出现在横轴上，另一个变量的值出现在纵轴上。数据中的每个个体都显示为图中的一个点。

367 **explanatory** /ɪkˈsplænətri/ **variable** 解释变量

- 英 variable that may help explain or predict changes in a response variable
- 释 解释变量是解释或预测响应变量变化的变量。
- 同 independent variable 自变量

368 response variable 反应变量

- **E** variable that measures an outcome of a study
- **释** 反应变量是衡量研究结果的变量。
- **同** dependent variable 因变量

369 positive /ˈpɒzətɪv/ association /əˌsəʊsiˈeɪʃn/ 正相关

- **E** When above-average values of one variable to accompany above-average values of the other and also of below-average values to occur together.
- **释** 正相关是指当一个变量高于平均值时，另一个变量也高于平均值；一个变量低于平均值时另一个变量也低于平均值。

370 negative association 负相关

- **E** When above-average values of one variable tend to accompany below-average values of the other.
- **释** 负相关是指当一个变量高于平均值时另一个变量低于平均值。

371 regression /rɪˈɡreʃn/ line 回归线

- **E** line that describes how a response variable y changes as an explanatory variable x changes; Use a regression line to predict the value of y for a given value of x.
- **释** 回归线是描述响应变量 y 如何随着解释变量 x 的变化而变化的线。使用回归线来预测给定 x 的 y 值。

372 least-squares regression line 最小二乘回归直线

- **E** the line that makes the sum of the squared vertical distances of the data points from the line as small as possible
- **释** 最小二乘回归直线是使数据点与直线垂直距离的平方之和尽可能小的直线。

373 **extrapolation** /ɪkˌstræpəˈleɪʃn/   *n.* 外推法

- **E** use of a regression line for prediction far outside the interval of values of the explanatory variable x used to obtain the line; Such predictions are often not accurate.
- **释** 外推法即利用回归线来预测远超出解释变量x取值范围的直线，这样的预测往往是不准确的。

374 **residual** /rɪˈzɪdjuəl/   *n.* 残差

- **E** difference between an observed value of the response variable and the value predicted by the regression line, residual = observed y - predicted $y = y - \hat{y}$
- **释** 残差是响应变量的一个观测值与回归线预测值的差值，即：残差 = 观测值y - 预测值 $y = y - \hat{y}$。

375 **residual plot**   残差图

- **E** scatterplot of the residuals against the explanatory variable; Residual plots help us assess whether a linear model is appropriate.
- **释** 残差图是残差对解释变量的散点图。残差图用于评估线性模型是否合适。

376 **coefficient** /ˌkəʊɪˈfɪʃnt/ **of determination** /dɪˌtɜːmɪˈneɪʃn/   确定系数

- **E** fraction of the variation in the values of y that is accounted for by the least-squares regression line of y on x; We can calculate using the formula $r^2 = 1 - \dfrac{\sum \text{residuals}^2}{\sum (y_i - \bar{y})^2}$.
- **释** 确定系数是x上y的最小二乘回归线所解释的y值变化的一部分。可使用公式 $r^2 = 1 - \dfrac{\sum \text{residuals}^2}{\sum (y_i - \bar{y})^2}$ 来计算。

377 influential /ˌɪnfluˈenʃl/ observation　　影响点

E An observation is influential for a statistical calculation if removing it would markedly change the result of the calculation. Points that are outliers in the x direction of a scatterplot are often influential for the least-squares regression line.

释 影响点是剔除影响统计计算结果的观测值后，会使统计计算结果发生显著变化的观测值。散点图的 x 方向离群的点通常对最小二乘回归线有影响。

第七小节　Designing Studies 设计研究　★（仅 AP 掌握）

扫一扫
听本节音频

378 census /ˈsensəs/　　*n.* 人口普查

E study that attempts to collect data from every individual in the population

释 人口普查是一项试图收集人口中每个人的数据的研究。

379 sample survey　　抽样调查

E study that uses an organised plan to choose a sample that represents some specific population; We base conclusions about the population on data from the sample.

释 抽样调查即有组织地来选择代表特定人群的样本的研究，根据样本的数据得出关于总体的结论。

380 inference /ˈɪnfərəns/ about a population
关于总体的推论

E conclusion about the larger population based on sample data; Requires that the individuals taking part in a study be randomly selected from the population of interest.

释 关于总体的推论是基于样本数据得出的关于较大总体的结论。要求从感兴趣的人群中随机选择参与研究的个人。

381 **population** /ˌpɒpjuˈleɪʃn/   *n.* 总体；人口

- 🄔 In a statistical study, the entire group of individuals we want information about.
- 🄚 在统计研究中，总体是指我们想了解的整个群体。

382 **convenience** /kənˈviːniəns/ **sample**   便利样本

- 🄔 sample selected by taking from the population individuals that are easy to reach
- 🄚 便利样本是从容易接触的人群中选取的样本。

383 **voluntary** /ˈvɒləntri/ **response sample**
自愿回应样本

- 🄔 People decide whether to join a sample by responding to a general invitation.
- 🄚 自愿回应样本是人们通过响应一般邀请来决定是否加入某个样本。

384 **random sampling**   随机抽样

- 🄔 using a chance process to determine which members of a population are included in the sample
- 🄚 随机抽样利用随机过程来确定样本中包含哪些人口。

385 **simple random sample**   简单随机抽样

- 🄔 Sample chosen in such a way that every group of n individuals in the population has an equal chance to be selected as the sample.
- 🄚 简单随机抽样即人口中每组 n 个个体都有同样被选为样本的机会。

386 **stratified** /ˈstrætɪfaɪd/ **random sample**

分层随机样本

- 🇪 sample obtained by classifying the population into groups of similar individuals, called strata, then choosing a separate SRS (simple random sample) in each stratum and combining these SRSs to form the sample
- 🇨 分层随机样本是将群体划分为相似个体的群体，称为阶层，然后在每个阶层中选择一个单独的 SRS，并将这些 SRS 组合起来形成样本。

387 **cluster** /ˈklʌstə(r)/ **sample**

聚类样本

- 🇪 sample obtained by classifying the population into groups of individuals that are located near each other, called clusters, and then choosing an SRS of the clusters; All individuals in the chosen clusters are included in the sample.
- 🇨 聚类样本即通过将群体分成彼此相邻的个体组（称为聚类），然后选择聚类的 SRS 来获得样本。样本中包含所选集群中的所有个体。

388 **observational** /ˌɒbzəˈveɪʃənəl/ **study**

观察性研究

- 🇪 study that observes individuals and measures variables of interest but does not attempt to influence the responses.
- 🇨 观察性研究是观察个体和测量感兴趣的变量，但不试图影响反应的研究。

389 **experiment** /ɪkˈsperɪmənt/

n. 实验

- 🇪 a study in which researchers deliberately impose treatments on individuals to measure their responses
- 🇨 实验是一项研究人员故意施加治疗措施，以衡量他们的反应的研究。

390 **confounding** /kənˈfaʊndɪŋ/   *n.* 混淆

- **E** When two variables are associated in such a way, their effects on a response variable cannot be distinguished from each other.
- **释** 混淆即当两个变量已相关联时,它们对响应变量的影响无法相互区分。

391 **experimental** /ɪkˌsperɪˈmentl/ **units**   实验单位

- **E** smallest collection of individuals to which treatments are applied
- **释** 实验单位是用来处理的个体的最小集合。

392 **subject** /ˈsʌbdʒɪkt/   *n.* 实验对象

- **E** experimental units that are human beings
- **释** 实验对象即人类作为实验单位(来被研究)。

393 **comparison** /kəmˈpærɪsn/   *n.* 比较

- **E** experimental design principle; Use a design that compares two or more treatments.
- **释** 比较是一种用于比较两个或多个处理对象的实验设计方法。

394 **random assignment** /əˈsaɪnmənt/   随机分配

- **E** experimental design principle; Use chance to assign experimental units to treatments. Doing so helps create roughly equivalent groups of experimental units by balancing the effects of other variables among the treatment groups.
- **释** 随机分配是一种利用机会将实验单元分配给处理对象的实验设计方法。这样做有助于通过平衡处理组之间其他变量的影响来创建大致相等的实验单元组。

395 **control** /kənˈtrəʊl/   *n.* 控制

- ☒ experimental design principle that mandates keeping other variables that might affect the response the same for all groups
- ㊟ 控制是一种保持可能影响所有组的响应的其他变量相同的实验设计方法。

396 **replication** /ˌreplɪˈkeɪʃn/   *n.* 复制

- ☒ experimental design principle; Use enough experimental units in each group so that any differences in the effects of the treatments can be distinguished from chance differences between the groups.
- ㊟ 复制即在每一组中使用足够的实验单元,以便将处理效果中的任何差异与偶然差异从各组中区分的实验设计方法。

397 **completely randomised** /ˈrændəmaɪzd/ **design**   完全随机设计

- ☒ design in which the experimental units are assigned to the treatments completely by chance
- ㊟ 完全随机设计是指将实验单位完全随机分配给各处理方案的设计。

398 **placebo** /pləˈsiːbəʊ/   *n.* 安慰剂

- ☒ inactive (fake) treatment
- ㊟ 安慰剂是无效的(假的)治疗方法。

399 **placebo effect**   安慰剂效应

- ☒ the fact that some subjects respond favourably to any treatment, even an inactive one (placebo)
- ㊟ 安慰剂效应即一些受试者对任何治疗都有良好的反应,即使是无效的治疗(安慰剂)。

400 **double-blind** /ˌdʌbl ˈblaɪnd/   *adj.* 双盲的

- **E** of an experiment in which neither the subjects nor those who interact with them and measure the response variable know which treatment a subject received
- **释** 在双盲实验中，实验对象和与他们互动并测量反应变量的人（研究者）都不知道他们接受了哪种治疗。

401 **single-blind** /ˈsɪŋl ˈblaɪnd/   *adj.* 单盲的

- **E** of an experiment in which either the subjects or those who interact with them and measure the response variable, but not both, know which treatment a subject received
- **释** 在单盲实验中，实验对象或与他们互动并测量反应变量的人（研究者）只有一方知道他们接受了哪种治疗。

402 **randomised block design**   随机区组设计

- **E** experimental design begun by forming blocks consisting of individuals that are similar in some way that is important to the response; Random assignment of treatments is then carried out separately within each block.
- **释** 随机区组设计即试验设计是通过形成由对响应很重要的相似个体组成的区组开始的，试验处理在各区组内随机排列。

403 **block** /blɒk/   *n.* 块

- **E** group of experimental units that are known before the experiment to be similar in some way that is expected to affect the response to the treatments
- **释** 块是一组实验单位，在实验之前就被认为在某种程度上是相似的，这可能会影响对治疗的反应。

404 inference /ˈɪnfərəns/ about cause and effect 关于因果关系的推论

- 🄴 conclusion from the results of an experiment that the treatments caused the difference in responses; It requires a well-designed experiment in which the treatments are randomly assigned to the experimental units.
- 🄲 关于因果关系的推论是从实验结果中得出的结论，即治疗方法引起了反应差异。这需要精心设计的实验，并将治疗方法随机分配给实验单位。

405 lack of realism /ˈriːəlɪzəm/ 缺乏现实性

- 🄴 When the treatments, the subjects, or the environment of an experiment are not realistic. Lack of realism can limit researchers' ability to apply the conclusions of an experiment to the settings of greatest interest.
- 🄲 缺乏现实性是指治疗、实验对象或实验环境不现实。缺乏现实性会限制研究人员将实验结论应用于最感兴趣的场景的能力。

406 institutional /ˌɪnstɪˈtjuːʃənl/ review /rɪˈvjuː/ board 机构审查委员会

- 🄴 board charged with protecting the safety and well-being of the participants in advance of a planned study and with monitoring the study itself
- 🄲 机构审查委员会负责在计划的研究之前保护参与者的安全和幸福，并监督研究本身。

407 informed /ɪnˈfɔːmd/ consent /kənˈsent/ 知情同意

- 🄴 basic principle of data ethics that states that individuals must be informed in advance about the nature of a study and any risk of harm it may bring; Participating individuals must then consent in writing.
- 🄲 知情同意是数据伦理的基本原则，规定必须事先告知个人研究的性质及其可能带来的任何危害风险。同时，参与的个人必须以书面形式同意。

408 **confidential** /ˌkɒnfɪˈdenʃl/ — *n.* 保密

- 🅔 a basic principle of data ethics that requires that individual data be kept private
- 🅡 保密是数据伦理的基本原则,即个人数据保持隐私。

第八小节 Probability and Random Variable
概率和随机变量 ★(仅 AP 掌握)

409 **law of large numbers** — 大数定律

- 🅔 If we observe more and more repetitions of any chance process, the proportion of times that a specific outcome occurs approaches a single value, which we call the probability of that outcome.
- 🅡 大数定律是指如果我们观察到任何偶然事件的出现次数越来越多,则特定结果发生的次数比例接近单一值,也就是称其为该结果的概率。

410 **simulation** /ˌsɪmjuˈleɪʃn/ — *n.* 模拟

- 🅔 imitation of chance behaviour, based on a model that accurately reflects the situation
- 🅡 模拟是根据准确反映情况的模型对偶然事件的模仿。

411 **probability model** — 概率模型

- 🅔 description of some chance process that consists of two parts, a sample space S and a probability for each outcome
- 🅡 概率模型是对偶然事件的描述,该过程由两部分组成:样本空间 S 和每个结果的概率。

412 **sample space** — 样本空间

- 🅔 set of all possible outcomes of a chance process
- 🅡 样本空间是偶然事件所有可能结果的集合。

413 **independent** /ˌɪndɪˈpendənt/ **random variables**
独立随机变量

E If knowing whether any event involving X alone has occurred tells us nothing about the occurrence of any event involving Y alone and vice versa, then X and Y are independent random variables.

释 如果知道是否单独发生了涉及 X 的任何事件，也并不能知道关于是否单独发生了涉及 Y 的任何事件，反之亦然，则 X 和 Y 是独立随机变量。

414 **discrete** /dɪˈskriːt/ **random variable**
离散随机变量

E a fixed set of possible values with gaps; The probability distribution of a discrete random variable gives its possible values and their probabilities. The probability of any event is the sum of the probabilities for the values of the variable that make up the event.

释 离散随机变量是一组有间隙的固定可能值。从离散随机变量的概率分布可以得出它的可能值及其概率。任何事件的概率是组成该事件的变量值的概率之和。

415 **continuous** /kənˈtɪnjuəs/ **random variable**
连续随机变量

E variable that takes all values in an interval of numbers; The probability distribution of a continuous random variable is described by a density curve. The probability of any event is the area under the density curve and above the values of the variable that make up the event.

释 连续随机变量是在一个数字区间内取所有值的变量。连续随机变量的概率分布用密度曲线来描述。任何事件的概率是密度曲线下的面积和组成该事件的变量的值以上的面积。

416 binomial /baɪˈnəʊmiəl/ setting — 二项式设置

E Arises when we perform several independent trials of the same chance process and record the number of times that a particular outcome occurs.

释 当我们对同一随机过程进行几次独立试验并记录某一特定结果出现的次数时，就需要进行二项式设置。

417 binomial random variable — 二项随机变量

E the count X of successes in a binomial setting

释 二项随机变量是在二项条件下成功的次数 X。

418 10% condition — 10% 条件

E When taking an SRS of size n from a population of size N, check that $n \leq 1/10\,N$.

释 10% 条件是指从大小为 N 的总体中获取大小为 n 的 SRS 时，请检查 $n \leq 1/10N$。

419 normal approximation /əˌprɒksɪˈmeɪʃn/ to a binomial distribution /ˌdɪstrɪˈbjuːʃn/ — 二项分布的正态近似

E Suppose that a count X of successes has the binomial distribution with n trials and success probability p. When n is large, the distribution of X is approximately Normal with mean np and standard deviation '$np\,(1-p)$'. We use this approximation when $np \geq 10$ and $n\,(1-p) \geq 10$.

释 二项分布的正态近似是指假设成功次数 X 具有二项式分布，其中 n 次试验且成功概率为 p。当 n 大时，X 的分布近似为正态，均值为 np，标准偏差为 "$np\,(1-p)$"。当 $np \geq 10$ 且 $n\,(1-p) \geq 10$ 时，使用此近似值。

420 large counts condition 大计数条件

- **E** It is safe to use Normal approximation for performing inference about a proportion p if $np \geq 10$ and $n(1-p) \geq 10$.
- **释** 大计数条件是指如果 $np \geq 10$,$n(1-p) \geq 10$,则可使用正态近似对比例 p 进行推论。

421 large counts condition for a chi-square /ˈkaɪskweə/ test 卡方检验的大计数条件

- **E** It is safe to use a chi-square distribution to perform calculations if all expected counts are at least 5.
- **释** 卡方检验的大计数条件是指如果所有的期望计数都至少为5,则可使用卡方分布进行计算。

422 geometric /ˌdʒiːəˈmetrɪk/ setting 几何设置

- **E** Arises when we perform independent trials of the same chance process and record the number of trials it takes to get one success. On each trial, the probability p of success must be the same.
- **释** 当我们对相同的概率过程进行独立试验并记录试验次数以获得一次成功时,就需要进行几何设置。在每一次试验中,成功的概率 p 必须是相同的。

423 geometric random variable 几何随机变量

- **E** the number of trials to get a success in a geometric setting
- **释** 几何随机变量是在几何环境中成功的试验次数。

第九小节 Sampling Distribution 抽样分布 ★（仅 AP 掌握）

扫一扫
听本节音频

424 **statistic** /stə'tɪstɪk/   *n.* 统计量

- 🇪 number that describes some characteristic of a sample
- 🇨 统计量是描述样本特征的数字。

425 **population distribution**   种群分布

- 🇪 giving the values of the variable for all the individuals in the population
- 🇨 通过种群分布可以得出种群中所有个体的变量值。

426 **sampling distribution**   抽样分布

- 🇪 the distribution of values taken by a statistic in all possible samples of the same size from the same population
- 🇨 抽样分布是指统计量在来自相同总体的相同大小的所有可能样本中所取值的分布。

427 **biased** /'baɪəst/ **estimator** /'estɪˌmeɪtə/ 偏倚估计量

- 🇪 a statistic used to estimate a parameter is biased if the mean of its sampling distribution is not equal to the true value of the parameter being estimated
- 🇨 偏倚估计量是一种用于估计参数的统计量，如果其采样分布的平均值不等于所估计参数的真实值，则该统计量存在偏倚。
- 🇷 unbiased estimator 无偏估计量

428 central limit theorem 中心极限定理

[E] In an SRS of size n from any population with mean m and finite standard deviation s, when n is large, the sampling distribution of the sample mean x is approximately Normal.

[释] 对于任意具有均值 m 和有限标准差 s 的 SRS，当 n 较大时，样本均值 x 的抽样分布近似正态。

第十小节 Estimating with Confidence 置信估计 ★（仅 AP 掌握）

扫一扫
听本节音频

429 point estimator 点估计量

[E] statistic that provides an estimate of a population parameter

[释] 点估计量是提供种群参数估计量的统计量。

430 point estimate 点估计

[E] specific value of a point estimator from a sample

[释] 点估计是样本中点估计值的特定值。

431 confidence /'kɒnfɪdəns/ interval 置信区间

[E] success rate of the method for calculating the confidence interval; In *C*% of all possible samples, the method would yield an interval that captures the true parameter value.

[释] 置信区间即计算置信区间的方法的成功率。在所有可能样本的 *C*%中，置信区间将产生一个捕获真实参数值的间隔。

432 margin /'mɑːdʒɪn/ of error 误差范围

[E] The difference between the point estimate and the true parameter value will be less than the margin of error in *C*% of all samples, where *C* is the confidence level.

[释] 误差范围是点估计与真实参数值之间的差将小于所有样本的 *C*%的误差范围，其中 *C* 是置信度。

433 **random assignment** 随机分配

E experimental design principle; Use chance to assign experimental units to treatments. Doing so helps create roughly equivalent groups of experimental units by balancing the effects of other variables among the treatment groups.

释 随机分配是一种利用偶然机会将实验单元分配给处理对象的实验设计方法。这样做有助于通过平衡处理组之间其他变量的影响来创建大致相等的实验单元组。

434 **random condition** 随机条件

E the data come from a well-designed random sample or randomised experiment

释 随机条件是精心设计的随机样本或随机实验的数据。

435 **standard error** 标准误差

E When the standard deviation of a statistic is estimated from data, the result is the standard error of the statistic.

释 用数据估计统计量的标准差,得到统计数据的标准误差。

436 *t distribution* /ˌdɪstrɪˈbjuːʃn/ t 分布

E Draw an SRS of size n from a large population that has a Normal distribution with mean μ and standard deviation σ. The statistic has the t distribution with degrees of freedom $df = n-1$. This statistic will have approximately a t_{n-1} distribution if the sample size is large enough, i.e. $t = \dfrac{\bar{x} - \mu}{\frac{s_x}{\sqrt{n}}}$.

释 从一个具有均值 m 和标准差 s 的正态分布的大种群中提取一个规模为 n 的 SRS。统计量具有自由度 $df = n-1$ 的 t 分布。如果样本量足够大,则该统计量的分布大约为 t_{n-1},即:$t = \dfrac{\bar{x} - \mu}{\frac{s_x}{\sqrt{n}}}$。

第十一小节 Testing a Claim 检验要求 ★（仅 AP 掌握）

扫一扫
听本节音频

437 significance /sɪɡˈnɪfɪkəns/ test 显著性检验

[E] procedure for using observed data to decide between two competing claims (also called hypotheses); The claims are often statements about a parameter.

[释] 显著性检验是使用观察到的数据来决定两个相互竞争的主张（也称为假设）的过程。主张通常是关于参数的声明。

438 null /nʌl/ hypothesis /haɪˈpɒθəsɪs/ 原假设

[E] Claim we weight evidence against in a significance test. Often the null hypothesis is a statement of 'no difference.'

[释] 原假设即在显著性检验中权衡证据。零假设通常是“无差异”。

439 alternative /ɔːlˈtɜːnətɪv/ hypothesis 备择假设

[E] the claim that we are trying to find evidence for in a significance test

[释] 备择假设是试图在显著性检验中寻找证据的主张。

440 one-sided alternative 单侧对立假设

[E] an hypothesis that states that a parameter is larger than the null value or that states that the parameter is smaller than the null value

[释] 单侧对立假设是表明一个参数大于或者小于空白值的假设。

441 two-sided alternative 双侧对立假设

[E] a hypothesis that states that the parameter is different from the null value (it could be either smaller or larger).

[释] 双侧对立假设是总体参数不同于（既可以大于又可以小于）空白值的假设。

442 *p*-value /piːˈvæljuː/   *n. p* 值

E The probability, computed assuming is true, that the statistic would take a value as extreme as or more extreme than the one actually observed, in the direction specified by H_a. The smaller the *p*-value, the stronger the evidence against H_0 and in favour of H_a provided by the data.

释 假设为真，则计算得出的概率将沿 H_a 指定的方向采用与实际观察到的值相同或更高的值。*p* 值越小，则针对 H_0 的证据越有力，并且证明了数据提供的 H_a 越强。

443 statistically /stəˈtɪstɪkli/ significant
统计学意义上的显著性水平

E (1) observed effect so large that it would rarely occur by chance; (2) If the *P*-value is smaller than alpha, we say that the results of a statistical study are significant at level α. In that case, we reject the null hypothesis and conclude that there is convincing evidence in favor of the alternative hypothesis H_a.

释 统计学意义上的显著性水平是指（1）观察到结果概率非常低，几乎不可能发生。（2）如果 *P* 值小于 alpha，则可以说统计学研究的结果存在 α 显著性水平。在那种情况下，拒绝零假设并得出结论，则有令人信服的证据支持备择假设 H_a。

444 type I error   I 型错误

E Occurs if we reject H_0 when H_0 is true.

释 当 H_0 正确的时候，拒绝了 H_0 的话就是 I 型错误。

445 type II error   II 型错误

E Occurs if we fail to reject H_0 when Ha is true.

释 当 H_a 正确的时候，没能拒绝 H_0 的话就是 II 型错误。

446 **paired data** 配对数据

- **E** study designs that involve making two observations on the same individual or one observation on each of two similar individuals result in paired data
- **释** 配对数据是涉及对同一个个体进行两次观察或对两个相似个体中的每一个进行一次观察的研究设计会产生成对的数据。

447 **pooled (combined) sample proportion** /prəˈpɔːʃn/ 合并样本比例

- **E** The overall proportion of successes in the two samples is
$$\hat{p}C = \frac{\text{count of successes in both samples combined}}{\text{count of individuals in both samples combined}} = \frac{X_1 + X_2}{n_1 + n_2}$$
- **释** 合并样本比例即两个样本中成功的总比例为
$$\hat{p}C = \frac{两个样本中的成功计数合并}{两个样本中的个体总数} = \frac{X_1 + X_2}{n_1 + n_2}$$

448 **randomisation** /ˌrændəmaɪˈzeɪʃən/ **distribution** 随机化分布

- **E** N Distribution of a statistic (like $\hat{p}_1 - \hat{p}_2$ or $x_1 - x_2$) in repeated random assignments of experimental units to treatment groups assuming that the specific treatment received doesn't affect individual responses. When the conditions are met, usual inference procedures based on the sampling distribution of the statistic will be approximately correct.
- **释** 随机化分布是假定所接受的特定治疗不会影响个体反应时，N在重复随机分配实验单位给治疗组的统计量（如$\hat{p}_1 - \hat{p}_2$或$x_1 - x_2$）中的分布。当条件满足时，基于统计数据的采样分布的常规推理过程将大致正确。

449 **observed count** 观察数量

- **E** actual numbers of individuals in the sample that fall in each cell of the one-way or two-way table
- **释** 观察数量是样本中属于单向或双向表的每个单元的实际个体数。

450 expected count 预期数量

E expected numbers of individuals in the sample that would fall in each cell of the one-way or two-way table if H_0 were true

释 预期数量是 H_0 为真时，样本中落入单向或双向表的每个单元格中的个体的预期数量。

451 chi-square /ˈkaɪskweə/ distribution 卡方分布

E family of distributions that take only nonnegative values and are skewed to the right; A particular chi-square distribution is specified by giving its degrees of freedom.

释 卡方分布是仅采用非负值且向右偏斜的分布族，是通过给出自由度来指定特定的卡方分布。

452 chi-square statistic /stəˈtɪstɪk/ 卡方统计量

E measure of how far the observed counts are from the expected counts; The formula is

$$x^2 = \sum \frac{(\text{Observed} - \text{Expected})^2}{\text{Expected}}$$

where the sum is over all possible values of the categorical variable or all cells in the two-way table.

释 卡方统计量是观察计数与预期计数之间的距离的度量。公式为

$$x^2 = \sum \frac{(观测值 - 期望值)^2}{期望值}$$

其总和超过分类变量的所有可能值或双向表中的所有单元格。

453 sample regression /rɪˈgreʃn/ line 样本回归线

E least-squares regression line $\hat{y} = a + bx$ computed from the sample data

释 样本回归线是由样本数据计算得到的最小二乘回归直线 $\hat{y} = a + bx$。

454 population regression line 总体回归线

E regression line $my = a + bx$ based on the entire population of data

释 总体回归线是基于整个数据总体的 $my = a + bx$ 的回归线。

第三节
Mechanics 力学

扫一扫
听本节音频

第一小节　Kinematics 动力学

455 **distance** /ˈdɪstəns/   *n.* 距离

- 🅔 length of path between two points
- 🅡 距离是两点之间的路径长度。
- 🅨 displacement *n.* 位移
  - distance relative to a fixed point or origin in a given direction
  - 位移是在给定方向上相对于定点或原点的距离。

456 **scalar** /ˈskeɪlə(r)/   *n.* 标量

- 🅔 quantity having a numerical value but no assigned direction
- 🅡 标量是有数值但没有指定方向的量。
- 🅨 vector *n.* 矢量
  - quantity having a numerical value in an assigned direction, which may be negative
  - 矢量是在指定方向上有数值的量,可以是负的。

457 **speed** /spiːd/   *n.* 速度

- 🅔 rate of moving over a distance
- 🅡 速度是移动距离的速率。
- 🅨 velocity
  - rate of change of displacement
  - 速度是位移变化率。

458 **discontinuity** /ˌdɪsˌkɒntɪˈnjuːəti/   *n.* 不连续性

- 🅔 the state of not being continuous
- 🅡 不连续性即不能连续的状态。

459 **instantaneous** /ˌɪnstən'teɪniəs/ **velocity** /və'lɒsəti/
瞬时速度

- ⓔ the velocity at an instant, which is the gradient at a point on a displacement-time graph, usually just referred to as velocity
- ⓒ 瞬时速度是瞬间的速度，是位移–时间图上一点的斜率，通常简称为速度。

460 **instantaneous acceleration** /əkˌselə'reɪʃn/
瞬时加速度

- ⓔ the acceleration at an instant, which is the gradient at a point on a velocity-time graph, usually just referred to as acceleration
- ⓒ 瞬时加速度是瞬间的加速度，是速度–时间图上某一点的斜率，通常简称为加速度。

第二小节　Force 力

461 **force** /fɔːs/　　*n.* 力

- ⓔ influence on an object that can alter its motion
- ⓒ 力是对能改变物体运动状态的物体施加的影响。

462 **tension** /'tenʃn/　　*n.* 拉力

- ⓔ force in a string, or other connecting object, which provides a force in the direction of the string away from the object it is connected to
- ⓒ 拉力是绳子或其他连接物体上的力，使绳子远离它所连接的物体。

463 **compression** /kəmˈpreʃn/   *n.* 压力

- ❷ force in a rod or other connecting object, but not a string, which provides a force in the direction of the rod towards the object it is connected to
- ㊥ 压力是杆或其他连接物体（但不是绳子）上的力，是指杆向它所连接的物体所施加的力。

464 **thrust** /θrʌst/   *n.* 推力
                                         v. 插入，推挤

- ❷ the force provided by, for example, a rod when under compression, acting along the rod towards an object
- ㊥ 推力是像杆在压力状态下所产生的力一样的力，推力沿杆向物体的方向作用。

465 **resistance** /rɪˈzɪstəns/   *n.* 阻力

- ❷ force opposing motion possibly caused by the air or other medium through which the object moves
- ㊥ 阻力是可能由空气或物体通过的其他介质引起的反作用力。

466 **gravity** /ˈɡrævəti/   *n.* 重力

- ❷ attraction between two objects as a result of their masses, usually thought of as a force acting on an object towards the Earth
- ㊥ 重力是两个物体之间质量引起的引力，通常被认为是作用在一个物体上朝向地球的力。

467 **Newton's first law**   牛顿第一定律

- ❷ the principle that an object continues moving in the same direction at the same speed unless a net force acts on the object
- ㊥ 牛顿第一定律即除非有力作用在物体上，否则物体将继续以相同的方向以相同的速度运动。

468 Newton's second law — 牛顿第二定律

- the principle that the rate of change of momentum is proportional to force acting on an object, which leads to the equation $F = ma$ in the case where mass is constant
- 牛顿第二定律即动量变化率与作用在物体上的力成比例，在质量恒定的情况下可用方程 $F = ma$ 表示。

469 negligible /ˈneɡlɪdʒəbl/ — *adj.* 可忽略的

- small enough to be ignored for the purposes of the mathematical model
- 可忽略的即足够小的，对于数学模型而言可以忽略不计的。

470 light /laɪt/ — *adj.* 轻的

- having no, or negligible, mass
- 轻的即没有质量的，或质量可以忽略的。

471 resultant /rɪˈzʌltənt/ — *n.* 合力

- single force equivalent to the net total of other forces
- 合力等于其他力的净总和。

472 equilibrium /ˌiːkwɪˈlɪbriəm/ — *n.* 平衡

- state of an object when there is no net force acting on it
- 平衡是物体在没有外力作用时的状态。

473 normal contact force — 支持力

- influence of one object on another through being in contact or the force acts perpendicular to the touching surfaces
- 支持力是指一个物体通过接触而对另一个物体的影响，或者该力垂直于接触表面作用。

474 **reaction force** 反作用力

- E alternative name for normal contact force
- 释 反作用力是法向接触力。

475 **component** /kəmˈpəʊnənt/ *n.* 组成部分

- E the parts of a force acting parallel to given axes, usually two perpendicular axes
- 释 组成部分是平行于给定轴（通常是两个垂直轴）作用的（力的）部分。

476 **resolving** /rɪˈzɔlvɪŋ/ *n.* 分解

- E process of splitting forces into components in given (usually perpendicular) directions
- 释 分解是将力按给定（通常是垂直）方向分解为分力的过程。

477 **line of action** 作用线

- E the direction in which a force acts
- 释 作用线即力作用的方向。

第三小节　Friction and Connected Particles 摩擦和连接体

478 **friction** /ˈfrɪkʃn/ *n.* 摩擦力

- E force between two surfaces acting parallel to the contact between the surfaces, as a result of the roughness of the surfaces in contact
- 释 摩擦力是两个表面之间由于接触表面的粗糙度所致的平行于两个表面之间接触的力。

479 **rough** /rʌf/ *adj.* 粗糙的

- E having friction
- 释 粗糙的即有摩擦的。

480 **smooth** /smuːð/ — *adj.* 光滑的

- **E** having no friction
- **释** 光滑的即没有摩擦的。
- **扩** smooth pulley 平滑滑轮
  - a pulley for which the magnitude of the tension in a string passed over it is the same on each side of the pulley
  - 平滑滑轮是一种滑轮,其上经过弦中的张力大小在滑轮的每一侧都相同。

481 **limiting equilibrium** /ˌiːkwɪˈlɪbriəm/ — 极限平衡

- **E** When friction is at its maximum possible value, but there is no net force on the object.
- **释** 极限平衡即当摩擦力达到最大可能值但物体上没有净力时,会出现极限平衡。

482 **coefficient** /ˌkəʊɪˈfɪʃnt/ **of friction** — 摩擦系数

- **E** the ratio between the frictional force and the normal contact force when friction is limiting
- **释** 摩擦系数即限制摩擦力时摩擦力与法向接触力之间的比率。

483 **contact force** — 接触力

- **E** the combined effect of two objects touching, comprising two components: the normal contact force and friction
- **释** 接触力是两个物体接触的综合作用。接触力由法向接触力和摩擦力两个部分组成。

484 **on the point of slipping** /ˈslɪpɪŋ/ — 在即将滑动的那个点

- **E** state of an object when friction is limiting so that any increase in the force applied to the object will cause it to move
- **释** 在即将滑动的那个点即在限制摩擦力的情况下物体的状态,因此此时任何增加在施加物体上的力都会使物体运动。

485 Newton's third law 牛顿第三定律

[E] the principle that for every action there is an equal and opposite reaction

[释] 牛顿第三定律即对于每个动作，都有一个相等且相反的反应。

486 connected /kə'nektɪd/ objects 相连的物体

[E] objects that are attached together with forces acting between them

[释] 相连的物体是通过作用在它们之间的力而附加在一起的物体。

487 rod /rɒd/ *n.* 杆

[E] any light rigid connector joining two objects

[释] 杆是连接两个物体的任何轻的并且硬的连接物。

488 string /strɪŋ/ *n.* 绳子

[E] any flexible connector joining two objects; it can be in tension but not in thrust; it is assumed to be light and inextensible.

[释] 绳子是连接两个物体的任何柔性连接物；绳子可以处于紧绷状态，而不能处于推力状态；绳子是轻的、不可扩展的。

扫一扫
听本节音频

第四小节 Momentum 动量

489 momentum /mə'mentəm/ *n.* 动量

[E] the quantity of movement of a moving object, measured as its mass multiplied by its speed

[释] 动量是一个运动物体的移动量，用质量乘以速度来计算。

490 impact /'ɪmpækt/ *n.* 冲击力

[E] a collision or other interaction between two bodies

[释] 冲击力是两个物体之间的碰撞或其他相互作用。

491 conserve /kən'sɜːv/   *vt.* 保存，使守恒

- **E** unchanged, as in 'total momentum is conserved in an impact'
- **释** 保存即恒定不变，如"总动量在冲击力中守恒"。

492 coalesce /ˌkəʊə'les/   *vi.* 合并，结合

- **E** When two bodies join together in an impact and continue as one object.
- **释** 合并即两个物体撞击在一起并作为一个物体继续存在。
- **扩** coalescence *n.* 合并
  - the union of diverse things into one body or form or group
  - 合并是指多种多样的事物结合成为一体、同一形式或同一群体。

493 explosion /ɪk'spləʊʒn/   *n.* 激增

- **E** When a single object splits into two or more separate parts
- **释** 激增即一个物体分裂成两个或两个以上的独立部分。

第五小节 Work, Energy and Power 功、功率和能量

494 work done   作功

- **E** The work done by a force that causes an object to move along the line of action of the force is the product of the magnitude of the force and the distance the object moves in the direction of the force. It is a scalar quantity, measured in joules (J).
- **释** 作功即使物体沿着力的作用线移动的力所完成的功，即力的大小与物体沿力的方向移动的距离的乘积。作为标量，功以焦耳（J）为单位。

495 work done by gravity /'ɡrævəti/   重力做的功

- **E** The work done by the weight of a body when the body falls vertically. If the body has mass m and falls through a vertical height h then the work done by gravity is mgh and equal to the decrease in potential energy.

🔃 重力做的功是物体垂直下落时通过其重量完成的功。如果物体的质量为 m，并且跌落到垂直高度 h，那么重力做的功为 mgh，等于势能的减小量。

496 **work done against gravity**　克服重力做的功

🅔 The work done by the weight of a body when the body is raised vertically. If the body has mass m and rises through a vertical height h then the work done against gravity is mgh and equal to the increase in potential energy.

🔃 克服重力做的功是指当身体垂直举起时通过身体的重量完成的工作。如果物体的质量为 m，并上升到垂直高度 h，那么抵抗重力的功为 mgh，等于势能的增加量。

497 **kinetic** /kɪˈnetɪk/ **energy**　动能

🅔 the energy that a body possesses because of its motion; Calculated as half the product of the mass and the square of the speed.

🔃 动能是人体因运动而拥有的能量，等于质量与速度平方的乘积的一半。

498 **gravitational** /ˌɡrævɪˈteɪʃənl/ **potential energy**
　　　　　　　　　　　　　　　　　　　重力势能

🅔 the energy that a body possesses because of its position (in a gravitational field); The potential energy is the product of the weight and the height.

🔃 重力势能是物体由于其位置（在重力场中）而拥有的能量。势能是重量和高度的乘积。

499 **work-energy principle**　功能原理

🅔 For any motion the increase in kinetic energy is equal to the work done by all forces or the increase in mechanical energy is equal to the work done by all forces (excluding weight).

🔃 功能原理即对于任何运动，动能的增加等于所有力的功，或者机械能的增加等于所有力（不包括重量）的功。

500 **conservative** /kənˈsɜːvətɪv/ **force** 保守力

- 🄴 a force for which the work done in moving an object between two points is independent of the path taken
- 🄷 保守力是在两点之间移动物体所做的功不因路径的不同而改变的力。
- 🄵 non-conservative force 非保守力
  - any force for which the work done in moving a particle between two points is different for different paths taken
  - 非保守力是在两点之间移动一个质点所做的功因路径的不同而改变的力。

501 **dissipate** /ˈdɪsɪpeɪt/ *vi.* 消散 *vt.* 浪费

- 🄴 mechanical energy lost by being converted into non-mechanical energy, such as heat, sound and light
- 🄷 消散即通过转换为非机械能（例如热、声和光）而损失了机械能。

502 **power** /ˈpaʊə(r)/ *n.* 功率

- 🄴 the rate of doing work, measured in watts; The power generated by the engine of a vehicle is the product of the driving force and the speed at which the vehicle is moving.
- 🄷 功率是做功的速率，以瓦特为单位。汽车发动机产生的功率是汽车前进的驱动力和速度的乘积。

高频专业词汇索引

10% condition 10% 条件 191
68-95-99.7 rule 68-95-99.7 法则 179

A

absolute convergence 绝对收敛 166
absolute maximum 绝对最大值 164
absolute minimum 绝对最小值 164
acceleration 加速度 116
add 加 101
adjacent 邻边 126
alternating series 交错级数 166
alternative hypothesis 备择假设 196
amplitude 振幅 145
angle 角,角度 117
approximation 近似值,近似法 104
arbitrary constant 任意常数 152
arc 弧,弧形物 123
Argand diagram 阿根图 157
argument 辐角 157
arithmetic progression 等差数列 148
arithmetic 算术 100
arrangement 布置,整理 173
association 关联 177
asymptote 渐近线 116
average 平均,平均数 170
axis 轴,坐标轴 115

B

bar chart 柱状图 136
base vector 基向量 130
base 基数 143

basic angle 基准角 144
bearing 方位角 128
bias 偏差 135
biased estimator 偏倚估计量 193
binomial distribution 二项分布 173
binomial random variable 二项随机变量 191
binomial setting 二项式设置 191
binomial 二项式 147
bisector 平分线 113
bivariate 双变量的 138
block 块 187
box-and-whisker plot 箱线图 139
bracket 括号 106

C

calculator 计算器 106
calculus 微积分 149
Cartesian form 笛卡尔形式 157
categorical variable 分类变量 175
census 人口普查 182
central limit theorem 中心极限定理 194
centre 中心 121
chain rule 链式法则 149
chi-square distribution 卡方分布 199
chi-square statistic 卡方统计量 199
chord 弦 123
circle 圆 121
class interval 组距 170
class mid-value 组中值 170
class width 组宽 169
clockwise 顺时针方向的 127
cluster sample 聚类样本 184
coalesce 合并，结合 207
coded 编码的 171
coefficient of determination 确定系数 181
coefficient of friction 摩擦系数 205
coefficient 系数 147
colinear 共线的 132

column vector 列向量 129
common difference 公差 148
common ratio 公比 148
commutative 交换的 155
comparison test 比较检验 166
comparison 比较 185
complement 补集 134
completely randomised design 完全随机设计 186
completing the square 配方法，完全平方 109
complex conjugate 共轭复数 156
complex number 复数 156
component 组成部分 204
composite function 复合函数 112
compound angle formulae 复角公式 146
compression 压力 202
concave 凹面的 153
concavity 凹面 164
conditional convergence 条件收敛 166
conditional distribution 条件分布 176
conditional probability 条件概率 136
cone 圆锥体 125
confidence interval 置信区间 194
confidential 保密 189
confounding 混淆 185
congruence 全等 120
connected objects 相连的物体 206
consecutive 连续不断的，连贯的 107
conservative force 保守力 209
conserve 保存，使守恒 207
constant 常数 106
contact force 接触力 205
continuity 连续的 161
continuous data 连续数据 136
continuous function 连续函数 159
continuous random variable 连续随机变量 190
control 控制 186
convenience sample 便利样本 183
converge 收敛 149

convergent sequence 收敛数列 167
convergent series 收敛级数 167
coordinate 坐标 114
coplanar 共面的 132
correlation 相关，关联 138
cosecant 余割 145
cosine rule 余弦定理 128
cosine 余弦 127
cotangent 余切 146
cross-section 横截面 124
cube root 立方根 158
cube 立方体；三次幂 103
cubic equation 三次方程 158
cuboid 长方体 124
cumulative frequency graph 累积频数图 170
cumulative frequency 累积频数 138
cumulative relative frequency graph 累积相对频率图 178
cylinder 圆柱 124

D

decimal 小数 100
degree 次 141
denominator 分母 102
density curve 密度曲线 178
derivative 导数 149
determinant 行列式 130
diagonal 对角线 122
diameter 直径 122
dice 骰子 135
differential equations 微分方程 151
differentiation 微分 149
dimension 维 121
directly proportional 成正比 110
discontinuity 不连续性 160
discontinuity 不连续性 200
discrete data 离散数据 136
discrete random variable 离散随机变量 190
discriminant 判别式 140

disk 磁盘 164
dissipate 消散 209
distance 距离 200
divergent series 发散级数 167
divide 除，除以 102
dividend 被除数 141
domain 定义域 143
double angle formulae 倍角公式 147
double-blind 双盲的 187

E

element 元素 133
elementary event 基本事件 172
elimination 消元 107
empty set 空集 134
enlargement 放大 126
equidistant 等距的 128
equilibrium 平衡 203
equiprobable 等概率的 172
estimate 估计 104
Euler's formula 欧拉公式 167
Euler's Method 欧拉方法 163
even function 偶函数 159
even number 偶数 103
expectation 期望值，预期 172
expected count 预期数量 199
experiment 实验 184
experimental units 实验单位 185
explanatory variable 解释变量 179
explicit function 显函数 151
explosion 激增 207
exponential form 指数形式 157
exponential 指数函数 116
extrapolation 外推法 181

F

factor theorem 因式定理 142

factor 因数 141
factorial 阶乘 148
factorise 因式分解 108
fair 公平的 135
favourable 有利的，顺利的 172
five-number summary 五数概括法 178
flow diagram 流程图 130
force 力 201
formula 公式 146
fraction 分数 100
frequency density 频率密度 137
frequency table 频率表 137
friction 摩擦力 204
fundamental theorem of calculus 微积分基本定理 162

G

general solution 通解 151
geometric distribution 几何分布 174
geometric progression 等比数列 148
geometric random variable 几何随机变量 192
geometric setting 几何设置 192
gradient 斜率 114
graphical 绘画的，用图表示的 111
gravitational potential energy 重力势能 208
gravity 重力 202
grouped frequency table 分组频率表 170

H

half line 射线 159
half-life 半衰期 161
harmonic series 调和级数 167
highest common factor 最大公因数 106
histogram 直方图 137
hypotenuse 直角三角形的斜边 126

I

identity 恒等式 145

imaginary number 虚数 156
impact 冲击力 206
improper integral 反常积分 152
increasing function 增函数 150
independent event 独立事件 135
independent random variables 独立随机变量 190
indeterminate form 不定式 163
index 指数 109
inequality 不等式 111
inference about a population 关于总体的推论 182
inference about cause and effect 关于因果关系的推论 188
infinite function 界函数 160
influential observation 影响点 182
informed consent 知情同意 188
input value 输入值 112
instantaneous acceleration 瞬时加速度 201
instantaneous velocity 瞬时速度 201
institutional review board 机构审查委员会 188
integer 整数 102
integral 积分 152
integration by parts 分步积分法 154
integration by substitution 换元积分法 154
integration 积分 152
interest 利息 105
intermediate value theorem 介值定理 160
interquartile range 四分位距 139
intersect 相交 115
intersection 交叉，交叉点 109
intersection 交集 133
inverse function 反函数 112
inversely proportional 成反比 110
irrational number 无理数 103
iteration 迭代 154

K

kinetic energy 动能 208

L

L'Hôpital's rule 洛必达法则 163
lack of realism 缺乏现实性 188
large counts condition for a chi-square test 卡方检验的大计数条件 192
large counts condition 大计数条件 192
law of large numbers 大数定律 189
least-squares regression line 最小二乘回归直线 180
LHS (left-hand side) 左手边 145
light 轻的 203
limiting equilibrium 极限平衡 205
line of action 作用线 204
line symmetry 对称轴 119
linear programming 线性规划 111
linear 线性的 107
linearisation 线性化 165
locus 轨迹 159
logarithm 对数 143
long division 长除法 142
lower boundary 下限 169
lower quartile 下四分位数，Q1 138
lowest common multiple 最小公倍数 106

M

magnitude 大小 155
major segment 大弓形 124
many-one function 多对一函数 143
mapping 映射 142
margin of error 误差范围 194
marginal distribution 边际分布 175
mathematical model 数学模型 173
matrix 矩阵 129
mean value theorem 中值定理 162
mean 平均数 137
median 中位数 138
mid-point 中点 114
minor segment 小弓形 123

mode 众数 138
modulus 模 157
modulus 模数；绝对值 130
modulus-argument form 复数的模 - 幅角形式 157
momentum 动量 206
motion 动作 162
multiply 乘 101
mutually exclusive 互斥的 135

N

natural exponential function 自然指数函数 144
natural logarithm 自然对数 143
natural number 自然数 102
negative association 负相关 180
negligible 可忽略的 203
net accumulation 积累净额 165
net change 净变化 165
Newton's first law 牛顿第一定律 202
Newton's second law 牛顿第二定律 203
Newton's third law 牛顿第三定律 206
normal approximation to a binomial distribution 二项分布的正态近似 191
normal contact force 支持力 203
normal curve 正态曲线 174
normal distribution 正态分布 174
normal 法线 150
nth root n 次方根 110
null hypothesis 原假设 196
number line 数值轴 111
numerator 分子 102

O

observational study 观察性研究 184
observed count 观察数量 198
odd function 奇函数 160
odd number 奇数 103
on the point of slipping 在即将滑动的那个点 205

one-one function 一对一函数 142
one-sided alternative 单侧对立假设 196
one-way table 单向表 175
operation 计算 109
opposite 对边 126
optimisation 最优化 165
outcome 结果 134
outlier 异常值 171
output value 输出值 112
overestimate 高估 153

P

paired data 配对数据 198
parabola 抛物线 140
parallel 平行线 113
parameter 参数 151
partial fraction 部分分式 142
particular solution 特解 151
Pascal's triangle 帕斯卡三角，杨辉三角 147
percentage 百分比 105
percentile 百分位 138
perimeter 周长 121
period 周期 144
perpendicular bisector 垂直平分线，中垂线 114
perpendicular 垂直的 113
pie chart 饼状图 136
placebo effect 安慰剂效应 186
placebo 安慰剂 186
plane 平面 120
plot 绘图，描点 115
point estimate 点估计 194
point estimator 点估计量 194
point of inflexion 拐点 150
polar coordinate 极坐标 158
polar form 极坐标形式 158
polygon 多边形 118
polynomial 多项式 141
pooled (combined) sample proportion 合并样本比例 198

population distribution 种群分布 193
population regression line 总体回归线 199
population 总体；人口 183
position vector 位置向量 129
positive association 正相关 180
power 功率 209
power 幂 110
prime number 质数，素数 102
principal angle 主角 145
prism 棱柱 124
probability density function (PDF) 概率密度分布函数 174
probability distribution 概率分布 173
probability model 概率模型 189
probability 概率，可能性 133
product rule 乘积法则 150
proportion 比例，倍数关系 105
p-value p 值 197
pyramid 棱锥体；金字塔 125
Pythagoras' theorem 毕达哥拉斯定理，勾股定理 119

Q

quadrant 象限 144
quadratic equation 二次方程 108
quadratic expression 二次表达式 108
quadratic formula 二次公式 109
quadrilateral 四边形 117
qualitative data 定性数据 169
quantitative variable 定量变量 175
quartic equation 四次方程 158
quotient rule 除法法则 150
quotient 商 141

R

radian 弧度 144
random assignment 随机分配 185
random assignment 随机分配 195
random condition 随机条件 195

random sampling 随机抽样 183
random 随机的 172
randomisation distribution 随机化分布 198
randomised block design 随机区组设计 187
range 值域 143
ratio 比率 105
rational number 有理数 103
raw data 原始数据 169
reaction force 反作用力 204
reciprocal 倒数 106
reflection 反射 131
region 区间 134
regression line 回归线 180
regular polygon 正多边形 122
relative frequency 相对频率 172
remainder theorem 余式定理 142
remainder 余数 141
replication 复制 186
residual plot 残差图 181
residual 残差 181
resistance 阻力 202
resistant measure 抗测量 178
resolving 分解 204
response variable 反应变量 180
resultant vector 合成向量 155
resultant 合力 203
revolution 旋转 153
Riemann sum 黎曼和 162
rod 杆 206
Rolle's theorem 罗尔定理 162
rotation 旋转 119
rough 粗糙的 204

S

sample regression line 样本回归线 199
sample space 样本空间 189
sample survey 抽样调查 182
sampling distribution 抽样分布 193

scalar product 点积 155
scalar 标量 200
scale 比例 120
scatter graph 点状图 137
scatterplot 散点图 179
secant 正割 145
sector 扇形 123
segment 部分 123
segmented bar graph 分段条形图 176
selection 选择 173
self-inverse function 反身函数 143
separation 分离 152
sequence 数列 104
series 级数 104
set 集合 133
shaded area 阴影面积 122
shear 切变 131
shell 壳 165
side-by-side bar graph 并排条形图 176
significance test 显著性检验 196
significant figure 有效数字 104
similarity 类似，相似 120
simple random sample 简单随机抽样 183
simplify 简化 107
simulation 模拟 189
simultaneous equation 联立方程组 107
sine rule 正弦定理 128
sine 正弦 127
single-blind 单盲的 187
skew 歪斜的；异面的 156
skewed 歪斜的 171
slant height 斜高 125
slope field 斜率场 161
smooth 光滑的 205
speed 速度 200
sphere 球体 125
spreadsheet 电子数据表 137
square root 平方根 158

- square 正方形；二次幂 103
- Squeeze Theorem 夹挤定理 160
- standard deviation 标准差 171
- standard error 标准误差 195
- standard normal variable 标准正态变量 174
- stationary point 驻点 140
- statistic 统计量 193
- statistically significant 统计学意义上的显著性水平 197
- stem-and-leaf diagram 茎叶图 139
- stratified random sample 分层随机样本 184
- stretch 拉长 131
- string 绳子 206
- subject 实验对象 185
- subset 子集 133
- substitute 代替 108
- subtract 减 101
- summarise 概括 171
- surface area 表面积 125
- symmetry 对称 119

T

- t distribution t 分布 195
- tangent 切线 113
- tangent 正切 127
- Taylor series 泰勒级数 168
- Taylor's theorem 泰勒定理 168
- tension 拉力 201
- thrust 推力 202
- transformation 变换，变形 130
- translation 平移 131
- trapezium rule 梯形法则 153
- trapezoid rule 梯形法则 163
- tree diagram 树状图 136
- trial 试验 135
- triangle 三角形 117
- trigonometry 三角学 126
- two-sided alternative 双侧对立假设 196
- two-way table 双向表 175

type I error I型错误 197
type II error II型错误 197

U

union 并集 134
unit vector 单位向量 155
unity 一 159
universal set 泛集 134
upper boundary 上限 169
upper quartile 上四分位数，Q3 139

V

variability of statistic 统计数据的差异性 177
variable 变量 109
variance 方差 172
variation 变化 171
vector addition 向量加法 155
vector 向量；矢量 129
Venn diagram 维恩图 134
vertex 顶点 140
vertical asymptote 垂直渐近线 146
voluntary response sample 自愿回应样本 183

W

washer 垫圈 165
work done against gravity 克服重力做的功 208
work done by gravity 重力做的功 207
work done 作功 207
work-energy principle 功能原理 208